A Time to Mourn

A Story of Grief and How One Grieved

Maree S. VanDerzee

Lessons on What to Say and What Not to Say When Someone is Mourning

LIONHEART GROUP PUBLISHING
EATON, COLORADO

A Time to Mourn

A Story of Grief and How One Grieved
Maree S. VanDerzee

Without limiting the rights under copyright reserved below, no part of this publication may be reproduced, stored in or introduced into retrieval system, or transmitted, in any form or by any means (electronic, mechanical, photocopying, recording, or otherwise), including mediums not yet invented at time of publication, without prior written permission from both the copyright owner and the publisher of this book.

All images and copyrighted materials included in this book are the personal property of the author or the author has been given permission to use. The QRCs provided link to content and are used for educational and research purposes only. Per Copyright Disclaimer under section 107 of the Copyright Act 1976, allowance is made for "fair use" for purposes such as criticism, comment, news reporting, teaching, scholarship, education, and research.

For information regarding permission, email Lionheart Group Publishing: permissions@lionheartgrouppublishing.com

Cover by Sandra Miller

Hardcover ISBN: 978-1-938505-62-1

Paperback ISBN: 978-1-938505-61-4

Library of Congress Control Number: 2022935916

Text copyright © 2020 by Maree S. VanDerzee

First Edition ~ May 2022

10 9 8 7 6 5 4 3 2 1

Published by Lionheart Group Publishing, Eaton, Colorado, USA

Printed in the USA ~ All rights reserved.

Visit us on the web at www.lionheartgrouppublishing.com

To Those Grieving...to Those Supporting the Grieving

NAMASTE IS A WORD THAT is used in the beautiful country of India and at the end of yoga sessions. It is a word that represents the belief there is a divine spark in each of us. *Namaste* meaning is, "I bow to the divine in you." "I see you. I am you. I know you. I feel you."

As my hands are placed in the prayer symbol to my heart, to you I say, "Namaste."

I see you.

I know you have it in you to do this journey of grief. To find yourself at a space of living a whole life again.

I know you have it in you to be the biggest support for those in the mourning time.

I see you.

I am you.

Namaste.

Dedication

To my soul mate ~ you complete me.

To our girls, Emalee and Katelyn ~ you fill our hearts.

To my Sweet Ariann ~ I wouldn't have missed the dance. I would do it all again for just four sweet months with you. I would dance the dance with you. Feel the hurt and heartache to have that dance with you. I know you are the Wind Beneath My Wings. *You are my Strength. You are the Reason for going on. For enduring to the end.*

To have you in the End is the Greatest of all Rewards. The Sweetest Gift is knowing where you are. You are in His arms. And you're with the Son of God celebrating Christmas in Heaven.

I look forward to joining you there.

Table of Contents

To Those Grieving	iii
Introduction	xi
Like Fireweed may We Be	1
The Strength to Go On	9
Ariann's Story	15
Rebecca June Cottam's story	29
Step into Hope	35
Acceptance in Grief	43
Thriving in Grief, not Just Surviving	53
Rise Up	61
Connection in Grieving	71
Here's your Sign	83
Sympathy vs. Empathy	101
What should I Say?	115
Supporting this Grief	121
Stages of Grief	131
Firsts are SO NOT EASY	141
There is a Time for Therapy	147
What are You carrying in Your Backpack?	157
Finding your Purpose	165
God's Plan vs. My Plan	173
God Moments	185
Tender Mercies from God	193
The Atonement of Jesus Christ	207
An Eternal Perspective. What? How? Why?	217
Moving Beyond and Thriving Forward	229
Healing—from the Good of the Earth	237
Meditating into Your Greatness	257
It is Well with My Soul	269
About the Author	279

A Time to Mourn

A story of grief and learning that "There is A Time to Keep Silent and a Time to Speak." Ecclesiastes 3:1

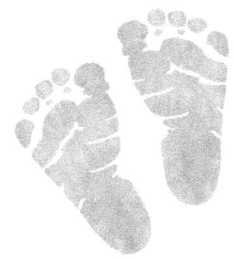 

Introduction

Ecclesiastes 3:1-8; "To everything there is a season, and a time to every purpose under the heaven: A time to be born, and a time to die; a time to plant, and a time to pluck up that which is planted; A time to kill, and a time to heal; a time to break down, and a time to build up; A time to weep, and a time to laugh; A time to mourn, and a time to dance; A time to cast away stones, and a time to gather stones together; a time to embrace, and a time to refrain from embracing; A time to get, and a time to lose; a time to keep, and a time to cast away. A time to rend, and a time to sew; a time to keep silence, and a time to speak; A time to love and a time to hate; a time of war, and a time of peace."

'Vs. 11 "He hath made everything beautiful in his time."

THERE IS A TIME TO mourn…and a time to keep silent as others mourn, yet to show up and speak truth and light when souls are mourning. This book is meant to teach you how to do and be that for others, and the story behind it all.

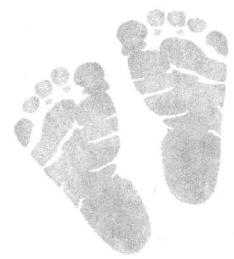

* 1 *

LIKE FIREWEED may WE BE

"Fireweed is the first thing to sprout, helping reestablish areas decimated by fire and deforestation." Wikipedia

I<small>N AREAS WHERE FIRES, FLOODS,</small> and devastation happens, there is a tenacious and beautiful wildflower called *fireweed*. It's the very first life to immediately return after the land has been devastated by a natural disaster.

The name 'fireweed' stems from its ability to create massive flowering growth in areas burned, by rapid fire. It was one of the first plants to appear after the eruption of Mount St. Helens in 1980, covering the fire-burned land. Known as *rosebay willowherb* in Great Britain, fireweed quickly colonized burned ground after the bombing of London in World War II, bringing beautiful color to an otherwise very grim landscape.

It's brought on and blooms after, because of disasters or uprooting of earth.

Isn't that amazing? I think so.

After trees regrow to shade the area, fireweed no longer gets enough sun to survive. So, it dies off. Yet the seeds stay alive in the ground, waiting for another forest fire or tragedy to pass through. When that happens, the seeds germinate and the fireweed flower grows and blooms once again. Through a tragedy, fireweed grows.

Fireweed grows in places where other plants do not intentionally grow. It's at home on riverbanks, sandbars, tundra, and roadsides. It blooms as grandly in gravel as it does on a mountain. Fireweed regenerates and transforms damaged soil. It can even sustain life by becoming food, drink, medicine, and warmth in times of an emergency. It is a tenacious and beautiful flowering plant.

I love the idea of it. 💡

Just when you think everything is lost, this bright, lovely flower appears above the ground to proclaim the survival of beauty and the continuation of life—even after some of the worst tragedies have hit.

It seems to be a true *Miracle* of Nature. Mother Earth's gift—brought in and given to us by the Creator of All.

I am inspired by fireweed. Can you tell?

For me, it's a symbol of hope, determination, and *thrival*. That's my word for thriving—not just surviving or survival, which is what most of us do after tragedy hits us.

But Thriving into THRIVAL! Like the fireweed. It's Thrival.

Fireweed is a message of, 'hold on, hope on, keep going, walk through it, and wait to see what is on the other side'. Just like a morning sunrise after a really dark, lonely, moonless night. This beautiful, flowering gift sprouts and blooms after the darkest and ugliest of the most devastating disasters.

Rising up like fireweed and finding hope is not easy after great loss and great heart break. Trust me, I know that kind of devastation. If you personally have experienced deep heartache, you know the kind of devastation I am talking about.

You might have also buried someone too close to you, suffered major heart trials, financial toughs, losses, divorces, natural disasters, and more.

Yet… sadly, I know.

I knew deep heartache at a young age.

I know how it feels to have the rug of life pulled out from under, left alone in a very dark place.

I know how it feels to lose someone; devastated so deeply.

I know how it feels to cry in the shower so no one can hear.

I know what it's like to 'fake' it and pretend it's okay, even though inside you are crying, screaming, "NO-PLEASE-NO!"

I know what it's like to wait for everyone to leave or fall asleep so you can fall apart, scream, and cry your eyes out.

I know what it's like to lay in bed all day and all night, sobbing for what no longer is.

I know what's it like to negotiate this 'bad dream' with someone, anyone. Begging, praying, and pleading for it to be different.

I know what it's like to cry at a grave over and over again, not knowing how to go on. Not wanting to go on.

I know what it's like to aimlessly be living life, not really even there.

I know what it's like to want to die. Begging to die.

I know what it's like to be done but can't take my own life. Just pleading for a car accident or a heart attack or something to take me, please.

I know what it's like and how it feels to be so broken I couldn't/didn't want to go on.

I've been there.

Maybe you have, too.

I know this because my precious, firstborn died early Christmas morning. We buried her two days later, on December 27th, which is when I felt deep devastation.

I was twenty-one years of age. Her father was twenty-three. The darkest of all nights for me was that Christmas night, thirty years ago. The darkest night of my soul.

The greatest loss a mother and father can experience is the loss of a child. The greatest burden and heartache for a mother to carry is to live life without one or more of her children. It doesn't just change you. It literally obliterates and then alters you for life. There is NO getting over it. You and your life are not EVER the same.

I truly believe you live life on another level after the loss of your child—a totally different level than those around you. They don't get it. They might never get it. It becomes life before and after burying a baby/child—divided into two parts because of the loss. Life and You, before the loss. Life and You, after the loss.

Losing a child is a place of complete survival, an indescribable journey you never want anyone else to experience, let alone yourself. Yet, it has happened to way too many of us—the Lost a Baby/Child Club. It really sucks to be in that club. Not a fun one. Babies/children ARE NOT SUPPOSED TO DIE BEFORE THEIR PARENTS! It's just not supposed to happen. Yet, it does.

To live it from the inside was the greatest intense pain and heartache I have ever known. Others I have spoken to feel the same. Living with it is unbearable at times. It's crazy, it's painful, it's heart breaking—and it feels hopeless and lonely.

To watch it from the outside looking in must be exceedingly difficult to do. I'm sorry for those of you who've had to do this or are doing this—watching us from the outside. Watching those you love go through that heartache must be very difficult. You don't know what to do or how to be there. Yet…You could make all the difference.

After the initial shock and numbness of loss, there's a time of complete shutdown—the, "How the heck-Almighty do I go on?" When grief has a tight grip on us, the chronic aching does not subside for a very, very, very long time. It's so hard to envision something other than complete despair in the moment, which is all there is in the very beginning. It's so difficult to know what to do with the 'crazy' feelings after a great loss and heartache in life.

I'd been through three divorces by the time I was forty-five. I have also had some *other* very personal and real tough heartaches. I have felt hopelessness, great pain, and the darkest of moonless nights, praying for the light and the sunrise to come.

People say to me, "You must be so strong to have gone through all you've gone through."

Bob Marley was quoted as saying "You never know how strong you are until being strong is the only choice you have." Sadly, for me, I *did not* know strong until there was no other way to be—when there was *no* other choice. It's just the only way for me to show up in those situations. Until you are in the trial of it, you don't know you're strong enough.

Did I know I had such tenacity and endurance for hard stuff?

I did not.

Did I think one HUGE, BURYING MY BABY trial was enough for me?

Yes, I did.

Have I had way more *hards* than I thought I should have?

Yes, I have.

Have I kept on going and thriving through them? Maybe. Maybe not. But I'm still standing, still persevering, still living my life to the best I know how. I am *thriving* in it now. Yet... it has taken *so very much* for me to get here.

My trial(s) might be a bit different than yours. Your story is definitely unique from mine. Yet, maybe we are similar in life, feeling devastation and huge heartache as we try to find our way through it.

Maya Angelou once said, "You may encounter many defeats, but you must not be defeated." Right?

The question is: How do we *rise up* from the demolished life we have and let the natural growth of fireweed come out—blooming beautiful and hearty in our lives? Just like fireweed in nature, beauty naturally grows in us after the ugliest of times. We just have to wait for it. Patiently. Waiting through the grief.

As the title of this book says and from *Ecclesiastes 3:4*, "...a time to mourn." And, it's okay to do so. I give us all permission to do so as we see fit.

Remember though, we all have the gift of the fireweed in us. It *is* in all of us. I recognize and honor the fireweed within you—and celebrate the fireweed within me, and within all. It grows up beautifully and naturally after the darkest and desolate of hours. *Always*!

The symbol of fireweed means there is *Hope, Determination,* and a *Thriver* in each of us, even after the great losses and heartaches of our lives. The fireweed will show up. Trust in that.

The fireweed is ready to burst through the seed with a new beauty, with a new path, with a new way of living and a new life—sadly, without your loved one. Your NEW life's normal— 'the new norm' as it's been labeled. Sad and crappy as it is, this is it. This is your road to travel, to find life again, and to see beauty in that journey—the road in finding the strength and courage to go on. It's in you. It's in all of us. I know it.

"Be strong and of a good courage, fear not, nor be afraid of them: for the LORD thy God, he is that doth go with thee; he will not fail thee, nor forsake thee." (Deuteronomy 31:6)

Journaling Thoughts

A Time to Mourn

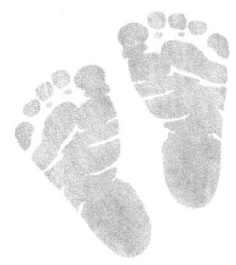

* 2 *

THE STRENGTH to GO ON

"The world breaks everyone and afterward many are strong at the broken places." ~ Ernest Hemingway

IF YOU LOOK AROUND, MANY are dealing with so much *broken*. We just finished the years 2020 and 2021. Quite a couple of years, right? Yet, that's where *strength* happens—in the *broken* of our lives or years. Even broken crayons still color. They make coloring pretty, despite being broken.

Being broken still works in people, too. The heart will break but even being broken, it keeps on working. Somehow the heart takes strength to keep beating and keep working despite the brokenness. Sometimes you don't even know from where it comes—the strength to go on.

I remember people saying to me, "I don't know how you are doing this," or "How are you surviving this?"

What choice did I have? What choice do we have when life's *hards* hit us?

I guess we have a choice in times of such *hard*—times of death, times of trials. We could choose out. Yet…I didn't know what else to do. Even as broken as I was after the death of my baby, I didn't know anything else but to go on—push through it and live—as much as I didn't want to live without her. There were times I thought about taking my own life. But at those times, the strength or the will to really choose *out* never came.

Strength sometimes does not come from looking like you're winning. Strength comes in simple ways. Waking up, getting up, and going through the motions in the mourning of it. Our struggles and heartaches in those times develop our strengths. When we go through our heartbreaks and choose not to surrender to the dark, that *is* strength. Strength at those times came from *One* for me.

God is my strength. He is the one who walks us through and will strengthen us in our broken hearts and in our trials. It takes strength in God to truly make your way through grief—to grab ahold of life and let it pull you onward and upward. Great strength to endure comes from Him.

The strongest people are not those who show their strength, but those who deal with pains and heartaches in their own lives while most of us don't know anything about what they're going through. I honor that strength. We have that in us. Many are going through stuff right now that pulls all the strength they know they can muster. It's that kind of beautiful strength which inspires me.

As I look around today, many are dealing with some seriously hard times and yet are finding the strength to endure. How are they doing it? Most say in the Lord. Some say through and because of their family or someone else. Some will say they don't know how they're doing it.

"The Lord will give strength unto His people; the Lord will bless His people with peace." (Psalms 29:11)

That's what we need to pray for in hard times—in times of loss, hurt, and heartache. Times we don't feel like we can go on in our strength. We need to ask, "Lord strengthen me to do this and give me peace to be with thy Will."

Is there a well of unlimited-strength water?

Yes! It is God's strength and it's the way we pull through grief.

Finding the strength through others around us can help, too. Finding those we can rely on for support and even those who've walked this journey and know this pain of loss we feel. It truly helps to reach out to people we can be honest with when we hurt. The important part is we aren't holding it all in. We're talking about how we feel. We're letting others help us if we need it.

I offer this prayer from the Reverend Laura Biddle:

O gentle and graceful spirit, I trust that you are a light in whatever darkness I bring to this moment. Help me open myself to hope, even as hopelessness has a grip. Grant me eyes to see the unending beauty of your creations, a heart softened enough to feel the everlasting presence of love, and a soul that can accept this loss and trust in the spirit of this hopefulness.

Ahhhhh, I love that. My light in the darkness, bringing me hope, with eyes to see and a heart that is soft to feel love, trust, and acceptance in my soul even during time of loss.

One of my greatest healing tools beyond Jesus, is music. I love music. It speaks to my soul—my broken soul and my whole soul.

As I listened to a Whitney Houston song many years ago, *I Didn't Know My Own Strength* it hit me hard. I didn't know *my* own *strength*, until *my* own strength was all there was to keep me going.

It takes great strength to make your way through grief, to grab on and let yourself be pulled up, pulled forward into a new life without the one you lost. "You never know how strong you are until being strong is your only choice." Finding your strength after great loss is a bold choice in life. A very bold choice. I hope you find your strength in whatever you are dealing with.

I want you hear the words of this song and listen to the power behind it. I really want you to blast it right now and take it in.

I'll wait as you pull it up and listen to the heart of this song, with your whole soul feeling it.

How did that feel? Did you feel it? *Ahhhh*—I love that song. I relate to those words and her heart as she says, "I thought I would never make it through," or "I had no hope to hold on to," and "There were so many times I wondered how I would get through the night."

That song *so* does it for me when I'm wondering how to continue and go on. I don't think any of us really know our own strength until we look back and say, "Wow, I did it! I made it through that one."

I didn't break and I did make it through after losing my baby (and a few more hurts) not so gracefully or pretty at all. But I kept going and made it through.

Maxwell Diawuoh said,

> *Even now, as broken as you may feel, you are still so strong. There's something to be said for how you hold yourself together and keep moving, even though you feel like shattering. Don't stop. This is your healing. It doesn't have to be pretty, or graceful. You just have to keep going.*

My suggestion to you is to make Whitney's song a part of your daily play list. Crank it up and feel the soul of the words in the song. Stepping into your *strength* as you get up and find a bit of hope, a bit of healing, and a bit of life again.

"Be strong and take heart, all you who hope in the Lord." (Psalms 31:24)

I hope you find hope in your heart and the *hope* in the Lord with the strength to go on.

Journaling Thoughts

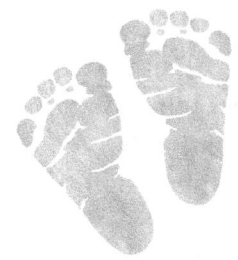

* 3 *

Ariann's Story

"I loved you from the very start. You stole my breath and my heart. Our life together had just begun, even though it was done. You are always a part of me, little one. No one else will ever know the strength of my love for you. After all, you are one of the only ones who knows what my heart sounds like from inside." Mom

Let me tell you my story, and about the sweet baby who gave me the *biggest heart trial*.

December 1989 - December 24th, 1990

We were so excited to be pregnant. So excited. We had been married over a year and we felt it was perfect timing. We thought we were ready for it all.

I loved being pregnant. I loved every minute of it. I loved feeling her inside of me—moving, filling up my belly with her sweet soul. I would have kept her in there forever if I could have.

It was a hot summer in St. George, Utah. 115 degrees *hot*. I would come home from my job and just lay my large pregnant self in a tiny kiddy pool of cold water—like a big whale hanging out in a tiny water source. Just trying to cool off.

My pregnancy with Ariann went so well. I did everything I could to eat healthy, not drink soda or take medicine...I felt I really wanted to give her the very best chance I possibly could. I felt good and so positive around birthing her. Even though she was my first pregnancy.

I didn't know how labor was *supposed* to go but, this one seemed to go quite nutty. I had stomach pains all day long and felt like I was coming down with the flu. I kept cramping and felt so queasy—flu-like queasy. But nothing that felt like contractions, just more cramping and upset tummy-like.

That evening I walked to the gas station around the corner from our home to get a *7-up* for my uneasy stomach. Nothing I did eased it. At 11:00PM, as I walked around, water gushed out of me.

I immediately called my mother-in-law. She told me my water had broken and I needed to get to the hospital. I woke up my husband. As he struggled to dress, I then felt the full pains of labor.

We lived thirty minutes from the nearest hospital. As he drove, with each intense labor pain I tightly squeezed his leg, making him push the gas pedal down even more—speeding the whole time to get there.

It was a really difficult delivery, as she seemed to have gotten stuck in my birthing canal due to a bone spur we had no idea was there. It was quite nutty. Our labor doctor was so good, he was finally able to pull her out by draining my bladder, positioning me differently, and then, with full force (using all his might and forceps), out she came. Coned head and beautiful. So angelic. A pure angel straight from God.

Ariann Maree Jacobs was born August 19, 1990, at 2:27 PM. She was an unbelievably gorgeous baby. I fell so hard in love—forever.

The beautiful precious life they placed in my hands took my breath away and quickly stole my heart. She was perfect.

One of the sweetest journal entries I wrote at the time of the birth said this:

August 19th, 1990

> *She is here. Oh my gosh—She is so beautiful. She has a bit of a cone head but she'll get over that. She has tons of dark black hair and she is dark skinned like me. She has a slight scratch on her cheek and behind her ear from the forceps having to pull her out. I am just sitting here looking at her and I am in awe. She is so precious and purely gorgeous. We made this little beauty. I had dozed for a minute and awoke to see her daddy in the chair, in the hospital asleep and her asleep on his chest. OH MY HEART. I am grateful for her in my life. She has all toes and fingers with all other parts working and she is a sleeping beauty who has graced our lives. How blessed are we because of her?*

Another journal entry a few months later said this:

> *Ariann is the cutest, sweetest, happiest, chunkiest baby ever. Everybody gushes at her. I mean, everyone gushes at her. She is so loved and adored. She draws attention like crazy and she loves the attention. Is this normal? Everyone stops, comments on her, and wants to touch her. She is that baby who draws you in, looks into your soul and you feel so much goodness with her. Pure Angelic. People are always stopping me when they see her, commenting on her, on her chunkiness, her light and her beauty. I don't quite understand this attention on her. Yet, she seems to be a gift to the world*

around us and she shares her light so generously and preciously. I love being her momma.

She was such a good baby. She loved smiling and laughing, and she did both so much. She didn't cry. She had such an angelicness about her all the time.

Throughout her four months of being with us, she had this funny thing she did. As I held her, feeding her or just sitting with her, she looked behind or to the side of me and would light up—as if she was seeing someone there. Then, she jabbered and baby-talked to whomever was there. She did that all the time. It was an interesting phenomenon I didn't think much about until after her death. *Hmmmm.*

* * *

I love Christmas. I love the decorations. I love the lights. I love the gifts—I love giving them. And I love getting them. I love the parties, the family gatherings. I love all the feels. All the Christmas goodies. I love it all. I *especially* love the music of Christmastime, the heart-felt songs and emotions they bring to me. Most of all, I *love* the meaning around Christmas, I love it!

I love the story in the bible of baby Jesus' birth. I love the salvation of Christ that was taught to me—that He brought to each one of us because of his birth. I absolutely love Christmas.

I was especially looking forward to our first Christmas as a new little family.

Ariann, me, and her daddy, together, celebrating that beautiful day. I was so excited, throughout the whole season playing the 'guess what's in this package' of our wrapped gifts with Ari and her dad. It was a fun and special time for me, as I absolutely loved the season.

Our last picture of her was taken at a church Christmas party on December 23rd. She sat on Santa's lap wearing an outfit that said, "What did Santa bring me?"

It is the most precious picture. I cherish it. I hang it on my Christmas tree every year.

She was chunky, happy, and full of life on Christmas Eve. We were all so excited to celebrate and honor the day we acknowledge as the Christ baby's birthday.

Sadly, celebrating it turned out to be quite the opposite for us. We put her to bed on Christmas Eve promising her the best First Christmas she would know. Even though at four months what would she know or remember? We still had great hopes for her and the future of Christmases with her.

* * *

I woke up early Christmas morning to silence and wondered why I was awake at that time. It was 2:33AM. I was always a good sleeper, so that was unusual. My husband and I were both wide awake and wondered why, so we just went about our Christmas morning preparation for the fun day, until about 7:00AM. I thought Ariann was 'having a sleep in', so I finally went into her room a bit after that.

She was wrapped up in a blanket and when I rolled her out, my heart and my mouth screamed, "She is dead!"

She was black and blue and stiff. I could see she had been gone for hours. My world crashed right then and there in that unreal moment on that early Christmas morning of 1990.

The memory of finding her in her crib and that harsh, heart-breaking morning has been forever etched in my mind.

Our angel baby girl was four months and six days when she died of SIDS in the early hours of Christmas morning, thirty-plus long and painful years ago.

Ariann Maree Jacobs forever in my heart, my mind, my soul—my heartache and my journey to find peace around her. For the rest of my life.

I think the toughest of all was the thought Ariann would miss out on this amazing gift of life, and I would miss out on Ari's life.

You always hope as a parent your child will be a happy and giving child—that you will get to live all their precious moments with them. To watch them crawl, walk, and run. Say their first word. Fall down. Lose their first tooth. Have chickenpox. Ride a tricycle and then a bike. Have a first day of school. See them be smart. Last day of school. Scholarships. College. Drive a car.

Date. Play some softball. Go to prom. Receive awards. Go on a mission. Get married. Have children. Have lots of babies. Live life to the fullest.

You see that in your kids even in the beginning—at least I did.

Yet, we got none of that. All gone in one blasted, ugly moment. None of that was in my plan for her future. That was one of the most difficult parts to swallow around losing her. The hope of her in my future—GONE! What the ????????

Did I sign up for this? I certainly did not think so, at that time.

When the first responders got there, they immediately said, "It's a SIDS."

I was twenty-one and didn't even know what SIDS was.

They say, "Sudden Infant Death Syndrome (SIDS) is the sudden unexplained death of a baby or child, usually less than one year of age." Years ago, they called it just SIDS, now they call it SUIDS (Sudden Unexpected Infant Death Syndrome) and a lot more unexplained deaths fall under that term.

Diagnosis requires the death remains unexplained, even after a thorough autopsy and detailed death scene investigation. SIDS usually occurs during sleep. But it just happens, and nothing can stop it from happening. No one to blame. No way of taking it back.

I have come to solidly believe in that. It *happened* and whether she had too many blankets, or a pillow, or overheated room...or they were on a bean bag, or made a brand-new down blanket, or was co-sleeping in bed—or anything else that added to the guilt of what was or wasn't done. It is what it is and what they declare it to be—Sudden and Unexplained death. *No one's* fault, no *ONE* to blame, *nothing* anyone *could have* or *should have* done. Step in to believing that!

Typically, a SUIDS death occurs between the hours of midnight and 9:00AM. There is usually no noise or evidence of struggle.

They told me it happens to preemies, underweight babies, sick babies, mostly boys, with smokers in homes, and in the winter months. Ariann was in only one of those categories—the winter months. Christmas morning.

Ariann was a chunky baby, weighing a whopping twenty-one pounds when she died. She was a healthy and a happy baby girl. Her well-baby check-up a few weeks prior went amazingly well. It didn't make any sense to me—none of it. I was reeling that Christmas morning instead of celebrating. Devastated. Heartbroken.

In 1990, there were 22,000 SIDS deaths in the United States and 119 of those were in Utah—my Ariann being one of those statistics. Sadly, it was one of the highest years for SIDS. I was one of 22,000 other U.S. parents that year who felt the sting, the emptiness, the aching arms (yes, that *is* real), and a huge hole in their hearts and in their lives. Yet, I felt all alone in that moment on Christmas day, and many more times after that day.

Sadly, SUIDS still happens way too much. I am now a part of a SUIDS *Facebook* group. It's heartbreaking to see and watch daily. SUIDS still takes the lives of many babies every year. There are numerous parents wondering what they could have, should have done to prevent it. Even though there is NOTHING, it doesn't stop the guilt, the heartache, and the devastation from the sudden death of the one we loved.

This was a post on the top of the group about SUIDS:

> *I wanted to share a bit with all of you since this board is for both SUID and SIDS parents. SUID stands for Sudden Unexpected Infant Death. Notice the U stands for unexpected, not unexplained. SUID includes both explained and unexplained deaths. Some examples of explained deaths include strangulation, suffocation, asphyxiation, and sudden illnesses that turned fatal. There are members on this board that lost their children to explained causes and it is necessary*

to recognize this fact. Those who fall into this category are welcome here. Their grief journey is very closely connected to those who lost their children to Sudden Infant Death Syndrome (SIDS). SIDS is a subset of the unexplained death. It is a death that typically occurs in a safe environment. There are no signs of strangulation, of suffocation, etc. Many medical examiners, especially in recent days refuse to label SIDS as a cause of death as the death really isn't a syndrome. They simply list the death as "undetermined" or "unexplained". All SIDS deaths are undetermined or unexplained. If a death has an explanation, it cannot be formally ruled SIDS. Sometimes there are secondary factors that are listed on an undetermined death. That means these factors could have factored into the child's death. One example is sleeping in an unsafe environment. If the primary cause is unexplained/undetermined then that means the medical examiner did not have evidence to make a definitive ruling. In other words, the death may or may not have resulted from that particular factor. Whether a member is here due to a SIDS loss or because of an explained (and unexpected) infant loss, they deserve respect and support. Trying to navigate the loss journey is a lifelong process.

Despite the little knowledge I had at that time, *all* I knew was my baby was gone. She had died in the early morning hours of Christmas. On the glorious day of the Savior's birth, my baby had been taken back.

Ariann Maree was our first born and we were so young. We were so naive about life, marriage, kids, and how to do it all. Yet, she was so loved. We had so much love for that sweet baby. I had so much love for her. *Now what?*

From the time I grew up, my belief was the first person to die in your life was supposed to be someone really old. I believed death only happened to someone who had lived a good life and was ready to pass on, naturally. I had not known death in my young life.

My very first funeral ever was my own four-month-old baby girl. That was a kicker. Funerals are one of the hardest events for me to attend, even now. I can count all the funerals I've been to on both hands since then. I can name exactly who they were, and how so very difficult it was for me to go to. I believe it's because of my very first experience with funerals—that one being so traumatic for me.

The experience with the paramedics and hospital was much better than most. I've heard horror stories of SUIDS happening in a moment and then the parents and family having to deal with cops bagging up baby's stuff, separating spouses. Homes become crime scenes, accusations, and much worst. I can't even imagine the confusion (on top of what I was bearing) to have to deal with that. Bless those souls who've dealt with that kind of crazy.

The people around me, *Praise God*, were very gracious—very mindful of us and our heartache that morning. They knew it was SIDS. They kept saying, "There is nothing you could have done," and "It happens a lot."

Our Christmas day was spent calling family and friends to let them know she had died, and planning a funeral for our precious, baby girl. That was the extent of our holiday—funeral planning and gathering family in.

UGH! Into the afternoon, I remember wanting to hold her after they took her from the hospital to the mortuary. Aching arms after a baby/child's death is so super real. They had sent her to Salt Lake City to have her autopsy, which was required.

I wanted to hold her and dress her for the funeral. I wanted last quiet moments with her. I wanted her back. I wanted it all back to normal. I sent a request into the mortuary to dress her for the funeral and to have one last moment with her before she was buried.

A person from the mortuary called and said, "You can come and hold her but they didn't do a good job sewing her back up after the autopsy, so we don't think you should dress her."

The idea of an autopsy was so disturbing to me. Imagining my sweet baby girl being cut into. *Oh Lord, help me and others dealing with this craziness!*

In the evening of the next day, we went to the mortuary to hold her. She was stitched all up her back into her head and around. But the smell, *Oh my gosh, the smell.*

I asked, "What *is* that *smell*?"

The guy at the mortuary said, "Embalming fluid."

"YUCK," I said.

After a few minutes of her being in my arms, I said, "This is not my baby anymore."

What I knew of my sweet, soft, yummy-smelling Ariann was no longer there.

She was gone.

It's devastating to look at the child you bore—watching her take her first breaths in your presence, come to full life—who no longer had any breathe of life or a Soul left in her. It was the first time in my young life to really *get* the power of the Spirit, the Soul that makes the living body. It's real. And without that Soul, there remains just a stiff, cold, smelly body. *Ugh!*

That was a harsh and real lesson for me.

Merry Christmas.

* * *

The next few days are a complete blur for me. Except one part of it… I would say, the hardest task I have ever done in my life was to pick out a casket for our baby girl to be buried in—a vessel that gets to hold our baby in the ground for a long time. Hard stuff.

Standing in the mortuary, looking at rows of super tiny, white, maroon, or pink, delicate caskets and screaming, "NOOOOOOOO! Please, NO!"

What a real harsh moment. I remember thinking, *I don't care, I don't want to do this!*

It was the first of many times in my life I would say, "I don't care, I don't want to do this."

I was beyond shocked. Not even in my right mind. The beginning of feeling like I was crazy. Henceforth began my Crazy Ride.

The viewing and funeral were somewhat of a blur. Unless something was said that triggered my pain and heartache, I don't remember much about it.

I do remember my little sister, Rebecca singing, "Families can be together forever, with Heavenly Father's plan. I always want to be with my own family, and the Lord has shown me how I can, the Lord has shown me how I can."

I do remember that moment. Interesting how that will come back around in our life. Rebecca, my baby sister, and that song.

Ariann Maree Jacobs was buried December 27th, 1990 in the St. George, Utah cemetery. It was a cold and dreary rainy day—exactly like my mood for a very long time. Looking back, I still have a hard time believing I survived it all.

My entry in my journal right after she died, said this:

January 7, 1991

Well—She is gone! Ariann Maree, our precious baby girl, died on Christmas morning. This is going to be the hardest thing of my life. I have lost the most precious and dearest gift of my life. She was my whole life, my bud, my heart, my world. I loved her so much. I have never been so hurt, so confused and so lonely in all of my life. Why? Why would God take something so special and dear to me? Am I being punished for all my past sins? I love her and I would have died for her. Why? Why Us? Why This? Why Christmas? It has been over two weeks and the pain and the heartache is not diminishing. My arms ache for her. It is too much to bear. My Mom stayed with us for a few weeks and she just barely left. My husband is back to work and I am alone. ALL ALONE. I ache for Ariann. Night times are really difficult. I am not sleeping. I wake up hearing her cry and I am trying to get to her but I can't find her. I have panic attacks every night now. The dreams are intense and harsh. Oh Ariann, do you know what Joy and Life you brought into our life? Do you know what pain and agony I am in now? Now what? I am so confused. How does one go on from this? Where and how do I begin to survive this great loss? Everyone keeps telling us we agreed to this, I don't know about that. I just do not feel comfort or peace. How do I go on?

That was difficult for me to re-read and yet, what I *do* know is that I *did* go on. I survived it. I found peace and joy again and now, years later, I have found Ariann every day in my life.

Ariann Maree is my forever angel. I hope from me sharing her story and this book you find peace and hope for yourself or for someone else. I am forever grateful I had her for the four months I did, as she deeply touched me in that time. She is forever my sweet baby girl and I lay hold of the promise that says, "All your losses will be restored to you in a time of your greatest joy." *Joseph Smith*

She was my greatest loss, and she will become my greatest joy someday. I hold on to that promise.

One of the lullabies I sang to my babies was *The Rose* sung by Bette Midler *(written by Amanda McBroom)*.

In memory of Ariann, I offer the words of that beautiful song reminding me of the many nights I sang her to sleep.

I have a tattoo on my ankle I got when I turned thirty. It has a yellow rose, wrapped around a purple butterfly—signifying my Ariann and my second baby, Emalee…

You are my butterfly, Ariann Maree—forever with me. Thank you, sweet angel girl.

You, Emalee, are my rose—the Bloom of Life after such loss.

* * *

Research assures us "… families can now live with the knowledge [SUIDs] was not their fault." Scan QRC to read entire report.

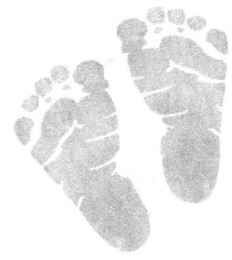

* 4 *

REBECCA JUNE COTTAM'S STORY

"You don't know love until you've carried a child. You don't know pain until you've lost a child." My mom

WHAT IS SO, SO NUTTY is that fourteen years to the date of healing my "stuff" around the death of my baby, we lost our little sister, Rebecca who was killed in a car accident. Fourteen years after Ariann's death, my mom faced the same hard—having to bury her baby girl.

Interesting how life gives us what it gives us. The baby of our family, Rebecca June Cottam was everyone's favorite. She was a fun, larger-than-life soul who we all loved and adored. She was twenty-one and had a potentially amazing future ahead of her.

She was on her way to college one early morning in January and was hit head-on and instantly killed. Difficult times again for the whole family. Watching my mom going through that intense, indescribable journey (even after going through my own) was super heart-breaking for me. I wanted to take it from her—make it better or right.

And yet, I could not. I couldn't take any of it from her. I had to let her walk in her own grief journey not knowing how it would go for her.

As I looked at my mom and her loss, I felt what she needed was that tiny bit of *hope* like I eventually found—A bit of fireweed.

Yet, my amazing, stout, Christian mom found her fireweed much quicker than I had. I saw *hope*—right after Rebecca's death—had come easily for her and had come from the true source of *hope*— Jesus Christ. It was because she knew Him so well and she had stayed connected with Him all her life, including during the time of the physical loss of her baby girl.

What was so amazing was watching my mom and my dad bear their grief right after. I knew they were closet criers, but to the world and in my perspective, they were faithful, strong, looked to God, and bore testimony of her new mission to complete strangers. They comforted her boyfriend and his parents during that time. They stood solid in what they knew to be true. It showed me how I could be in the face of great grief.

* * *

One of my sweetest and most tender last moments with Becca (a week before she died) was in my home. At 1:00AM my bedroom door opened up and I startled, only to find Becca standing there.

She said, "Maree, Can I sleep with you? Mom and Dad are gone, and I watched a scary movie, and I can't stay home alone."

She crawled into bed with me, and we talked until 5:00AM or so, and then slept for a few hours until we both had to get it up and get going.

I will hold tight to that memory until I see her again, and we have another beautiful night like that one.

My parents were in Hawaii when Rebecca passed. I can't even imagine that one. Having your kids call you on your first vacation away to tell you one of your children had been killed in a car accident. Hard stuff. Mom and Dad seriously found peace in Christ and their testimony of Him. Standing in who they knew Him to be for them, their Prince of Peace, the Healing Hands of Him that touched them as they endured their tragedy.

As my brother said, "They are prepared for this because of who they were and what they believed their whole lives. They prepared us for this because they taught us to believe and stand in that same foundation."

I do not think my parents ever swayed in their foundation because they built it upon *The Rock of Jesus Christ*. (Helaman 5:12)

One of the prayers of my heart with Becca's death was, "Oh Lord, teach me how to embrace this grief and to not fight it, so that I may experience the true healing that comes from you this time around."

Surprisingly, I felt so buoyed up by My Savior and Lord Jesus Christ in that big loss. I learned with Becca to mourn with Jesus Christ and to let Him heal me through it. I was so much stronger in my testimony of Jesus Christ in burying my sweet baby sister.

I share more of this in another chapter but to mourn in and through Jesus Christ is a different way of mourning big loss. There is a time to mourn and a time to mourn through and in our Savior, Jesus Christ. He brings peace, comfort, healing, and hope to anyone who is in their time of mourning.

* * *

Rebecca loved Josh Groban. We kept talking about going to a Josh Groban concert together. One of the songs that hit me after she died was his, *To Where You Are*. (Written by Richard Marx and Linda Thompson).

The words perfectly remind me of Rebecca, her beautiful smile, and her being not so far away from us.

I seriously love that sweet sassy sister of mine. She is always close, still. Even more so when I throw on some Josh Groban and blast it for her and me. And we dance together. She still laughs and hangs out with me and the ones she loves. I feel it. I love her. I miss her, and I know so much more because of the physical loss of her.

* * *

The sweet song that was sung by Rebecca and my nieces at Ariann's funeral, and then sung by our nieces and nephews at Rebecca's funeral is still touching to sing and hear. I hear of the Father's eternal plan when I hear the words, *Families Can Be Together Forever*.

* * *

Each of us will have our own Fridays—those days when the universe itself seems shattered and the shards of our world lie littered about us in pieces. We all will experience those broken times when it seems we can never be put together again.

We will all have our Fridays. But I testify to you in the name of the One who conquered death—Sunday will come. In the darkness of our sorrow, Sunday will come. No matter our desperation, no matter our grief, Sunday will come. In this life or the next, Sunday will come. ~ Joseph B Wirthlin

Sunday always comes and families are together forever. I am grateful to know this.

Journaling Thoughts

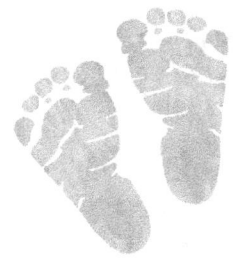

* 5 *

STEP into HOPE

Behold, you will sit in the radiant sun without sorrow, no longer seeking, searching for the magic that will make the pain go away—ready to hope, to love, to smile, to sing, to give, to heal again. And you will have stopped asking why." TO HEAL AGAIN *by Rusty Berkus*

IN MY EXPERIENCE, SOMETIMES AGAINST all devastation, all brokenness, all odds, all logic, with all that happens in life, there remains a small bit of *hope* in us. A tiny glimmer of it somewhere deep within all of us. It is there. It could take a certain moment, a person, or a sign for it to pop out.

Hope still comes up every day, just like the sun rising. Just like the growing fireweed. We might not see it in times, but it is there all around us, waiting for us to notice it.

The moon will rise in different shapes all month long, so often like our grief. Yet the sun rises as a large source of light the same way every morning. It's the representation of *hope*. The *light* that comes after the *darkest* of nights from the early morning sunrise.

We just have to wait for it, watch for it, and even patiently know it will come—especially in our obliterated lives, in our blackest of moonless nights. Hope is there.

> *Hope is the thing with feathers; that perches in the soul; and sings the tune without the words; and never stops—at all.* ~ Emily Dickinson

In the early beginnings of my baby's death, one of the things I found hope in was music. Music opened me up, made me cry, and left me feeling something again. A stirring in me. It was there—a small stirring of something inside of me touched by the sweet gift of music.

Trying to define hope is like trying to describe the feel of a gentle breeze. How do you describe the thin feeling of a steady but welcoming air, like a breeze? It's like trying to define faith or love. It is a bit difficult to do but it's just as real.

Hope is like that. Thin in the beginning.

I describe it as hope being light. It is a light within all of us that pierces the darkness of doubts and discouragement and taps into the *greatest* light (hope) of All Creation—even the Savior. Let's call it the Light of Christ. Hope, in a word, is our Savior, Jesus Christ. The Son of God. He is Hope.

Hope is a part of The Creator in all of us, and holds us tightly to Him. A simple thread. A thread connected to God, connected to Jesus Christ, connecting into us. Holding on to that thread is crucial in hard times.

The *hope*, for me, was so hard to feel and see in my tender early moments of losing Ariann. I did not feel *hope*. I felt *hopeless*. Such a loss of *hope*.

Somehow, somewhere in the midst of my heart trial, I saw *hope*. Just a small bit of hope. A bit of Christ showing up.

He can be that for us. Our *hope* to go on. Moments of tender graces, light in the dark, or someone else who can facilitate that hope for us. We all get to choose.

Will this test/trial make me strong or will it make me miserable and void of hope and life? It's a choice. *Will I let the hope in?*

What do you choose?

It was easier for me to feel that hope fourteen years later when my little sister, Rebecca was killed in that car accident. Maturity. I had already gone through a *real hard*. It takes some time, some work, and some stepping in to see and feel hope. Even again and again.

Hope. It might be there at one moment in time and then it feels gone. It shows up in a moment and then intense grief and heartbreak take over, and it's gone again—at least that's how it felt for me. Hope is so tender and fragile during heartbroken times. Flitting in and out.

I heard someone say, "Sometimes it's harder to hold on to hope than a moonbeam."

I imagine the light of Christ shining down into the top of my head, kind of like a thread of light. Letting that lighted thread stay within us is crucial at a time of feeling devastated. Hold on and see that thread intertwined with our God and Savior and with all humanity. No matter how fragile or thin the thread might be, it's always there, giving us hope. That tiny thread of a fireweed seed ready to open and bloom.

* * *

When my baby died, I tried to rely only on myself, and myself alone. At that point in my young twenty-one-year-old life, I had not tapped into that thread beyond myself—into the Savior himself. I did not know His power and His strength to help me through.

Sadly, there are far too many like me in the world. Especially in the past few crazy years.

Regrettably, we rely solely on ourselves in devastating times, thinking we can maybe get through it without anyone else. While it is good to be self-reliant, in the hardest of times we have to rely on our Savior, Jesus Christ—our hope of all hopes.

In this instance, we may be able to substitute the word *hope* for *light* and get some understanding in the scriptures. We talk about Christ as being the *light* of the world—he is also the *hope* of the world.

"When Jesus spake to the people, He said, "I am the light of the world. Whoever follows me will never walk in darkness but will have the light of life." (John 8:12)

Replace the word *hope* for *light*. That scripture would then say,

I am the hope of the world. Whoever follows me will never walk in darkness but will have the hope of life.

He is the *hope* of life—the *hope* of this world. Walking with Him we never walk in darkness, only hope in life.

Even though we're all living with different circumstances, the feeling of can't go on, hopelessness, and defeat can be heavy when we're in it the midst of it. It is dark and it feels like despair. There is nothing to look forward to.

When you're living in the devastation and feeling like you're living without hope, trying to cling to it in the darkest of times can be very difficult. I challenge you to step into God's promises.

"For I am the Lord, your God, who takes hold of your right hand and says to you, DO NOT FEAR; I will help you." (Isaiah 41:13)

"For I know the plans I have for you,' declares the LORD, 'Plans to prosper you and not to harm you, plans to give you HOPE and a future." (Jeremiah 29:11)

"...and this is the confidence that we have in Him, that, if we ask anything according to His will, he will hear us. And we know that he hears us, whatsoever we ask, we know that we have the petitions that we desired of Him." (1 John 5:14-15)

In so many scriptures He promises us He is there. He is the hope holding on to us. Even if we aren't holding on to Him. He will give us hope, peace, light, and love in times of need.

I know all too well about this. I was not holding on to Him when my baby died. Even after, I did not hold on to Him. Yet, He had me. My prayers were, "Bring her back", "Give her back to me." Not anything else.

That was not His will or way.

Yet, I know hope gives us the courage and strength to do what we don't think we're capable or strong enough to do. In the darkest of hours hope can find us. If we hold on, hope finds us.

* * *

In my years of camping out, hanging out in the middle of nowhere, I have seen the brightest and most amazing sky of stars appear in the darkest of places with no lights around. It's a brilliant sky of stars surrounded by complete darkness.

Only in the darkest of nights can you see the power of light and the many lights around you. It's there. Hope shines in.

Dr. Martin Luther King Jr said, "Only in the darkness can you see the stars." It's the promise of hope.

I have not yet lost a parent, so I don't know that pain. I have not lost a husband to death, so I have not felt that. I have said goodbye to a few husbands through divorce—those were dark times. I buried my baby way too soon. I've lost grandparents so I know that sorrow. Fourteen years after the death of my baby, we lost a baby sister at her young age of twenty-one. I know grief. I know loss. I know pain. I know hopelessness and I know finding hope.

It can even be just as difficult to watch those we know and love go through the painful, heartache-grief ride.

Jesus Christ *is the ultimate source of hope.* He is the way through. It is He who created the resilient fireweed and it is through Him we find that seeded thread of *HOPE* in us. Connected to Him. It is He who is saying, "Hold on to me, I am reaching for you. Keep trying in me. I love you. I will not leave you alone. It will be better, somehow. I promise."

Christ always is there for us. We must reach up to Him and His tiny thread of hope in us at our grieving time. We are able to overcome because of Christ and the hope He provides.

What I have learned through my pain is, hope is not about what we see in any situation, but about being able to see God no matter our situation. Knowing He is there, He is with us, He is holding tight to us, and sometimes through it all, as the famous *Footprints in the Sand* (by Carolyn Carty, Flora Haines Loughead) poem says, "He whispers, 'My precious child, I love you and will never leave you. Never, ever, during your trials and testings. When you saw only one set of footprints, it was then that I carried you.'"

He carried me. I just didn't see it. God is in all parts of our lives, including the grief and the healing in hope that comes after. To know God and his Son, Jesus Christ is to know hope in times of grief—to know fireweed will continually bloom because of them.

Paul wrote, "For our sakes, no doubt, this is written: that he that ploweth should plow in hope, and he that thresheth in hope should be partakers of His hope." (1 Cor 9:10)

We must plow in hope—and have that hope in reaping and partaking of His harvest. Even in our hardest, saddest moments of life. It's part of the growth and harvest—the ebb and flow of life. And when we plow in hope, stepping into hope, that's what we will reap. Hope. That is His promise. As hard as it seems it will be and can be, step into hope.

If you're in *the grief* right now, I ask you to begin to see fireweed waiting to bloom—the hope around you, in you, and the healing power of Jesus Christ in your life. He knows all. He provides the *tender mercies*. Wait and watch for them.

Dr. Martin Luther King Jr said, "We must accept finite disappointment but never lose infinite hope."

As you know, I love music. I believe music is the possibility for us to find transformational healing. Deep transformational healing for me comes through the soulful sound of music. Daily for me, music fills me with hope—with a new sense of possibility. It changes me. It fills me with light, it makes me cry, it makes me feel, it opens me up. I feel hope in songs of heart and inspiration, even messages of sadness and sorrow.

I love listening to music even in my darkest of nights. So throughout this book there are songs for you. Blast them–WAY LOUD! Hear them, I want you to *feel* what's being sung and spoken to you. Feel the music in you—giving you hope. I hope you find it in the music I share with you.

As this chapter ends, I share this song I love, love, love.

Hope in Front of Me, *written by James Brett / Herms Bernie / Gokey Danny and sung by Danny Gokey*

Blast it proud and loud as you see the hope in front of you.

* * *

Neal A. Maxwell said,

> *Real hope is much more than wishful musing. Hope is realistic anticipation taking the form of determination—a determination not merely to survive but to 'endure...well' to the end.*
>
> *In the geometry of restored theology, hope has a greater circumference than faith. If faith increases, the perimeter of hope stretches correspondingly. Hope keeps us 'anxiously engaged' in good causes even when these appear to be losing causes.*
>
> *Those with true hope often see their personal circumstances shaken, like kaleidoscopes, again and again. Yet with the 'eye of faith,' they still see divine pattern and purpose. Whatever our particular furrow, we are to 'plow in hope', without booking back or letting yesterday hold tomorrow hostage.*

I talk about *hope* in this chapter to prepare us all to begin to feel, see, and hear where *hope* is. Open up to *hope*. Feel *hope* and feel *light* in you as you mourn and support the mourning. I pray you and I may plow in *hope*, not allowing yesterday to hold tomorrow hostage.

JOURNALING THOUGHTS

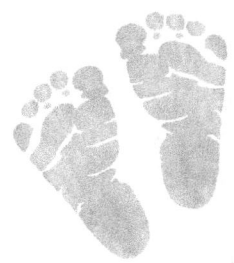

* 6 *

ACCEPTANCE in GRIEF

Accept—then act. Whatever the present moment contains, accept it as if you had chosen it. Always work with it, not against it. ~ Eckhart Tolle

From my experience hope, I believe, begins by stepping into acceptance. When death and loss hits us, acceptance seems to be difficult to come by. Or, so I thought.

When I look back at my most difficult times, acceptance was missing in the moments—including the death of Ariann. Remember my prayer, "Please give her back"? No acceptance there.

The first step I dealt with in my grief journey was the complete denial of the death of our baby. *Was it a dream? Did that really happen? When am I going to wake up? This can't be real.*

I remember screaming to myself after she died, "THIS CAN NOT BE REAL—GET ME OUT OF THIS DREAM!"

I certainly was not accepting it as it was. Who would want to? I sure didn't.

I felt as if I was stuck in a world without anything, with nothing to look forward to. I was screaming, "Help me!" inside but no one seemed to hear me. I really wrestled with a lot of the 'How?' and 'Why?' questions for some time in the beginning of my great loss. Normal grief.

Then comments made to me reminded me others were also not accepting what *was* and what *wasn't* in the moment. One of the first steps of grief is denial—not accepting what has been placed in front of us. Acceptance is a scary place to be because it means that *it's* real. Yet, let's look at what this word implies for us.

First, acceptance does not mean liking, wanting, choosing, or supporting the *truth* in front of us. By not accepting, we struggle in the pain and resist what is reality. When we choose to allow it to be as it is, it has an element of letting go of the resistance and stepping into the realness—the lesson in front of us.

I am big fan of Deepak Chopra's book, *The Seven Laws of Spiritual Success*. He dedicates one complete chapter (Law #4) to how we need to receive with open arms what happens to us. If we fight and resist it, we generate a lot of turbulence in our minds (especially with grief) and for those around us who love us and are watching us in our turbulent time.

Carl Jung said, "What you resist persists."

What is probably really difficult for some who support the griever, is looking at the grief-stricken and not knowing how to begin to help or how to be there at that time.

I remember my aunt saying to me one time, "I saw you sitting at her grave as I drove by and thought, 'What a difficult journey and I don't even know how to begin to be there for her.'"

Yet, she *was* there for me. She showed up. She talked to me about it. She let me find my way despite what she thought about the way I was grieving or what I was doing as I was going through it.

Some days there was a glimmer of light for me—small tokens of love, friendship, and hope. A bit of fireweed threading into my life. Some days there was no light, no moons, complete darkness—a large void and such intense, lonely pain. There were definitely many days it was hard to even get out of bed—nothing I could do to make things any better or ease it for myself.

I felt like I was on a crazy, intense emotional roller-coaster ride and no one, including myself, could get me off it. Up and down, my emotions went on this grief-ride for such a long time. I did not know how to control my emotions or even what to do with them.

Sadly, most of those around me did not know what to do for me, either. I know it was not easy for them to watch me struggle for so long.

My friend said one time she passed me on the road. I was driving the other way and it looked like I wasn't even there, as she waved and waved at me. People came to know they could find me sitting at Ariann's graveside, day in and day out. Some even told me it wasn't healthy for me or good for me moving forward.

I didn't know what else to do. So, I found myself sitting next to her grave every day. Just sitting there crying at her grave was all I could do in that moment on my grief journey. It felt normal and somewhat good for me at the time. And that was okay—for me.

It's not the same for others. Some can't even go to the grave and that's okay, too. Whatever is or isn't, is *just right*. Exactly as it should be.

But, for some reason, it didn't seem okay for those surrounding me and that made it even harder for me—being told what I should or shouldn't do or feel or shouldn't feel or say or shouldn't say.

The pain and sorrow we feel and know from death and heartache is because we loved so very deeply. That kind of love causes heavy mourning and deep sorrow. We loved deeply and that is good. We now mourn deeply and, in the only way we know how to, grasp and keep going on.

We have to learn how to lose deeply. We have to learn to heal from the pain of loving and losing so deeply. How do we do it?

We find a small bit of acceptance, a tiny inkling of hope and determination in us—an itty-bit of fireweed ready to burst from the seed and grow despite the tragedy of what goes on around us.

Even in the grief-denial and shock moments when you're saying, "Was there any other way", "Hope this is going to change, be different", "Wake up!", "God's hands will make it right." Whatever you're saying, it is the denial part of the grief journey, and it is okay. Acceptance is the next step from here. Acceptance takes some time and some hope.

Trusting it is a time to mourn, a time for finding hope and acceptance—which follows after.

Acceptance is a practice of living in the right *now*.

"Of course there is no formula for success, except perhaps an unconditional acceptance of life, and what it brings." ~Arthur Rubinstein

Acceptance is the first step in restoring hope. It will come. It just takes a dang thing called time and accepting that one, too. Believing it is what it is, as it is, and accepting life right then in that moment, is never easy.

Most people who've not yet dealt with grief have a hard time. It's okay that it's even more difficult in the midst of such heartbreak. To accept the moment right *now* definitely is a practice. This loss, this feeling, this emptiness, this sorrow, this despair is real for you. In this very moment, that's all there is. And it is okay. To accept it as it is seems to be through some divine grace, some moving into light and out of your deepest, darkest night of it.

How do we rise above accepting what is and what isn't?

Basically, one moment, one hour, one day at a time. Let me repeat: ONE MOMENT, ONE HOUR, AND ONE DAY AT A TIME!

It can be done, I promise.

Keep going on.

Keep feeling the lonely.

Keep feeling like you are in Hell.

Keep falling down.

Keep feeling like you are crazy.

Keep crying.

Keep walking backwards.

Keep being angry.

Keep crying.

Keep screaming.

Keep missing them.

Keep wishing for them back.

Keep bawling your eyes out.

Keep wanting to die.

Keep waking up.

Keep crying.

Keep hoping on.

Keep walking forward.

Keep missing them.

Keep looking up.

Keep grieving this loss.

Keep going.

Keep crying.

Keep reaching out.

Keep talking to someone about it all.

Keep knowing someone is listening.

Keep going.

Keep holding on.

Keep feeling the emotions because that means you're alive still and that's good.

Keep holding on to the hope of some fireweed in you.

You *will* get through this.

Getting through comes by leaning into the hurt, the grief and the pain, knowing it is actually truly meant to be this way. It was not an accident. There was nothing wrong. It was part of the plan. We are not broken, just a little bent and yet, we will come through. We *will* find our way.

There will be many lessons from this we will learn and grow through by grace we'll be grateful for, someday.

You will bounce back into your 'new' norm of life, like I did. Not the past life—it's a different one, sadly. One without the one you love. But it is this way. You will find the gift of acceptance. You will one day see fireweed grow like crazy all around you. You will feel acceptance rise, just as the large sun does every morning. You will see acceptance light up in your daily life. You will stand in hope. You will smile, you will laugh, and you will think fondly of the one you love.

And maybe you'll say like I do now, "I would do that again, just to have the moments I had with them—the short time we shared. I would do it all again."

I know that might sound crazy, even to those of you who are at the very beginning of this grief journey. But the grief eases, it lightens up. I promise. It never goes away, but it lessens the hold on your breath, on your heart, on your soul, and on your life.

There is a darling book my sister gave me a few months after my baby's death called, *To Heal Again: Towards Serenity and the Resolution of Grief,* by Rusty Berkus which says,

> *You sit in the shadow of sorrow seeking, searching for the magic that will make the pain go away. Weep what you must weep, not only for this loss, but for all other losses you have sustained in this life. Surrender into the memory of what once was and can no longer be. This winter of your life will pass, as all seasons do. Stay in your season of Winterness as long as you need be, for everything that you feel is appropriate.*
>
> *There is no right way to grieve—there is just your way. It will take as long as it takes. It is important to be ever so gentle, kind, loving and giving to yourself right now and to let others be ever so gentle, kind, loving and giving to you.*
>
> *Remember how deserving you are of gentleness, kindness, lovingness and givingness.*
>
> *No one ever said it was easy to let go, let be, let life do what it is supposed to do. Perhaps you feel you are the only one in the Universe. But out of your loss is an interconnectedness with all humanity— for you are ONE with everyone who has ever mourned.*
>
> *When you live fully, your vulnerability takes you through the shadows of winter where you feel you may never see the Sun again. To cease living fully because you fear the winter shadow is never to see the Sun at all.*
>
> *Judge not the appearance of this loss. Behind the darkest cloud of the dreary winter chill, is a springtime begging to burst forth. Bless this pain for it will bear its perfect gift to you in its perfect time.*

It longs to thaw the frozen winter of your grief. For the invisible world of the Spirit will be your greatest power with which to heal. Know beyond all knowing, that through the power of the Spirit within, you will befriend your highest self.

The exquisiteness of this Friendship leads you to realms of compassion, humility and service, to a fulfillment you never knew existed, into a Holy instant of springtime—of harmony, creativity and the opportunity to once again master your life.

Behold, you will sit in the radiant sun without sorrow, no longer seeking, searching for the magic that will make the pain go away, ready to love, to smile to sing, to give, to heal again.

And you WILL HAVE STOPPED ASKING WHY.

When I read this book, the end hit me the hardest, "...*and you will have stopped asking why."* That was what I wanted. That certainly sounds like the gift of acceptance. "There is no right way to grieve—just your way to grieve."

Remember that. Hold on to that. Accept that. Hope on to that.

And then you will have stopped asking why. Yep, this grief walk is the acceptance journey of stepping into hope.

The *Serenity Prayer* is the common name for a prayer written by the American theologian, Reinhold Niebuhr (1892–1971).

The original says, "God, grant me the serenity to accept the things I cannot change, the courage to change the things I cannot accept, and wisdom to know the difference."

When we are no longer able to change our circumstance, we are challenged to accept our current circumstances. We must learn to accept as we cannot change grief and loss. To accept is to step into God's plan and His will. To know there are no accidents—that it is exactly as it should be.

Our greatest example of acceptance is our Savior in Luke 22:42—"Father, if thou be willing, remove this cup from me: nevertheless not my will, but thine, be done."

Failing to accept reality—to accept what is in the moment creates suffering where there's already intense pain. It creates even more confusion where there *can* be clarity. It creates anguish where there *can* be peace.

We don't accept in order to change what's happened, nor do we do it in order to feel better about it. We accept because it's the only logical thing to do.

Whatever has happened, has happened. Whatever occurred already occurred. We embrace reality because it's already here, right now, and resisting it won't make it go away.

Learning acceptance is a lifelong process, and we're guaranteed to be given plenty of opportunities to practice acceptance in our life.

Accepting what God gives us in the moment and in the next moment is the biggest gift we can learn in life.

How can you baby-step into acceptance? Even if it's accepting what *is*, right now?

Could it be you accepting that you hurt and are at a loss of what to do or how to move forward?

Or accepting that you need a day to be alone? Or accepting you need people today?

What else is it you might accept in this moment in your journey? Just one step in to acceptance begins the journey.

Erich W. Kopischke said,
> *The ultimate source of empowerment and lasting acceptance is our Heavenly Father and His Son, Jesus Christ. They know us. They love us. They do not accept us because of our title or position. They do not look at our status. They look into our hearts. They accept us for who we are and what we are striving to become. Seeking and receiving acceptance from them will always lift and encourage us.*

Time for the famous song sung by Princess Elsa (Idina Menzel) in *Frozen* trying to accept herself as is…

Let it Go *(written by Kristen Anderson-Lopez and Robert Lopez)*

What can you let go of today that doesn't serve you? What can you hold on to that is important or serves you today?

JOURNALING THOUGHTS

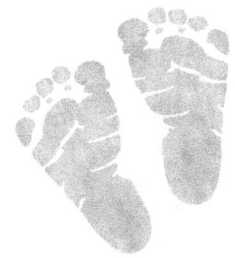

* 7 *

Thriving in Grief, not Just Surviving

"To any who may be struggling to see that light and find that hope, I say: Hold on. Keep trying. God loves you. Things will improve." ~ Jeffrey R. Holland

"Hold on. Keep trying." Keep being in just *one* moment—*one* hour and stepping into one day at a time. To those who despair and feel there is no hope, there is an assurance of the Psalmists words, "weeping may endure for a night [or two or three], but joy cometh in the morning." (Psalms 30:5)

Joy cometh in the morning.

Joy does come. Then guilt. Then joy. Then more guilt. Then light and joy come. Then less guilt. More joy. More peace. More guilt. More light. So on and so on.

It's up and down, but it just takes some time, some patience, some outside love and assistance from your people.

You will find your people—the one(s) you know who are your support crew or healing tribe. The one(s) you can trust, the one(s)

53

you can call, the one(s) who will show up and will be with you despite all you're going through in your grief journey. The one(s) who are truly there for us.

I have my one(s). Do you?

Holding on to hope is not as easy as it is stated, is it? Fear seems to be a driving master of this grief-life. Hope often seems to take the back seat.

That seemed to be the way for me, too, after my baby died.

Fear.

As my marriage ended, I found myself pregnant with my next baby, a single soon-to-be mom, barely breathing myself. And *I'm* supposed to be holding on to any kind of hope and a future?

Fear drove me at that time. It was painstaking for me to feel or hold on to hope. I felt so void, so empty, and so desolate in my life at that time of being alone.

I kept asking myself and others, "How do I find my way through this? How do I survive this great loss?"

I didn't know how to do it so I asked so many others.

How do we step into our lives after such tragedies have hit us—be it a death, a divorce, or hard trials of life?

The statement I shared in the last chapter is a difficult one to swallow sometimes, "When we are no longer able to change our current circumstances, we are challenged to accept our current circumstances." That was not easy for me after my loss.

We are no more able to change the circumstances of a divorce, a loss, a baby dying, a husband dying, a parent dying, a teenager dying, or even a grandparent dying than we can change how close (or not close) we are to dying. There is no way to change those circumstances no matter how hard we try, nor how much we want.

Accepting change in life is one of the hardest things to do. At least for me it was and still can be.

When we can't change events, it becomes the challenge to change us to accepting those circumstances and not just surviving—actually thriving in those circumstances.

I had to change me in my circumstances back then—change how I saw things, how I was being about it, and change my beliefs around certain ideas I had around my baby's death. I had to change *me* if I wanted to thrive. I knew it. I had to level up and learn to thrive.

Thriving in the circumstances of death, divorce, or any loss seems unheard of. Thriving is defined as flourishing, prospering, growing vigorously, and blossoming, making strides.

Maybe you ask. "How is that even possible in times like this?"

Can I share a few stories that inspired me to see thriving in life's circumstances?

The beautiful, country singer, Reba McEntire... Have you heard of her? A few months after my baby's death, on March 16, 1991 Reba went through what she calls the 'darkest hours' of her life. Following a show in San Diego, seven members of Reba's band and her long-time tour manager boarded a private jet to take off to their next tour stop. Reba stayed behind to sleep and recover from an illness.

Tragically, outside San Diego the jet's wing caught the edge of a rock on the side of a mountain. The jet crashed, killing everyone on board.

Can you even imagine Reba's devastation of losing eight of her "family" members? That's what band members call each other—Family. Reba questioned why they had to be taken so soon. I cannot even imagine what she was feeling through her great loss. Those souls had been with her from the beginning—for years, playing and working with her.

She said, "We will be marked by this crash forever."

Reba went on and created some of her biggest hits, releasing and dedicating her sixteenth album, 'For my Broken Heart,' in memory of the band members who were killed in that crash.

I remember laying in my bed after my baby died, listening to the title song of this album over and over and over and over again. And crying…

Listen to words from the song, *For my Broken Heart*:

Ahhhhhh… I still cry when I hear that beautiful song play.

There are so many things Reba could have done in her devastating loss—pulled in, shut herself up, not move on. Yet, she chose to thrive and honor the lives of those who had gone. She created hits that touched many lives and spoke to souls who were going through their own nightmares. Including me. That album is a tear-jerker and I love it to this day.

Scan the QRCode and cry—and feel the emotions as you step into being a *thriver*, like Reba.

Can I give you another example?

I love the beautiful and dynamic, Elizabeth Smart. Her story is one of heartache, triumph, and thriving.

As a fourteen-year-old innocent girl, she was kidnapped by a disturbed man and his wife. They did all kinds of unbelievable horrors to her at her young and innocent age.

Nine months later, she was found and had surprisingly survived all that the twisted couple did to her. She had experienced things no fourteen-year-old should ever even know of, much less experience.

She had lost so very much, including her virginity—her precious innocence, which was taken by him over nine months. She lost those nine months of her life. Surprisingly, she did not lose her mind. I can't even imagine her pain, heartache, and grief.

She inspires me.

The abduction of Elizabeth Smart was one of the most-followed child abduction cases of our time. In her riveting Ted[x] Talk, she discussed her abduction and encouraged, "When you're faced with a trial, don't give up, don't surrender. Move forward, because you will never know what you will do with it. Because you never know the lives you will be able to touch."

The day Elizabeth was found, her mom told her:

Elizabeth, what this man has done to you is terrible and there are not words strong enough to describe how wicked and evil he is. He has stolen nine months of your life you will never get back.

The best punishment you could ever give him is to be happy—to move forward with your life and to thrive in it. Because by feeling sorry for yourself, and holding on to the past, and dwelling on what's happened to you, that's only allowing them more control, more power, still more of your life away from you.

> *So don't let that happen. Justice may or may not be served. Restitution may or may not be made. But don't you dare give them another second of your life.*

What an amazing perspective her mother had. How many of us could have said that to our daughter after going through what she went through?

Her mom did. She totally inspires me. Elizabeth and her mother are powerful examples of acceptance in circumstances.

Elizabeth not only stepped into her circumstances and survived them, she thrived in the tragedies and heartaches given to her. She still is thriving. Heartaches don't stop. Life's hard.

Elizabeth has become a phenomenal example of thriving in life. Since her abduction, Elizabeth has gone on to become an advocate for missing children and for victims of sexual assault, opening after-care centers for exploited children. She has written a few books, has become an inspiring speaker, as she continues to share her story again and again.

Amazing, isn't it?

Those are a few examples of thriving in circumstances.

It takes some time—yes. A whole lot of compassion and some real searching in our heart, finding ourselves able to step into that thriving life instead of just surviving it.

I didn't do it so graciously when my baby died. Or, during some of the next trials in my life. But I keep working on it. That's what matters.

Elizabeth Smart's mom *got it*.

Beautiful words of affirmation to put on your mirror and to inspire into every day: "I am a thriver."

Elizabeth Smart's mom's advice, I share with you because as you read my story about my baby, you will see how much energy

I gave into the negative talk. Taking too many moments of my life being triggered by what was said and not being able to stand in acceptance. Barely surviving in my grief.

As I look back, I let so many of those grieving, heartbreaking moments keep me from not truly living my own thriving life. I was in 'barely survival' mode, after my baby died—and a few other times.

I have since learned and continue to learn as trials come up:

- What are the lessons to learn from this?
- How can I go from surviving to thriving in trials?
- What's the part I play in all of this?
- What's the story I am telling myself and others about all of this? Is it truth?

I am a thriver and so are you. That's what matters now, right? It's not easy in the midst of the biggest heartache of your life, I know. Yet it's possible to see it in someone else—and to see it in yourself. Thriving.

I am finally that! So are you! That's why I wrote this book—to give hope. I came through the biggest heartache (including two and three others) of my life, and so can you.

One of my favorite songs is Danny Gokey's, *Tell Your Heart to Beat Again* (written by Bernie Herms, Randy Phillips, and Matthew West).

Listen and crank it up.

I hope you can tell your heart to beat again and step into your great big life with all you're supposed to learn and grow from this. I hope you find that for you—for others in your life. For our losses.

Journaling Thoughts

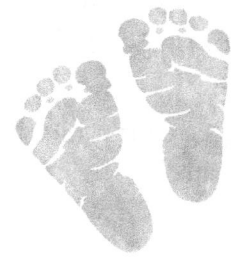

* 8 *

RISE UP

"Don't give up; rise up!" Maree

Y<small>OU WILL COME TO KNOW</small> I am a God girl. I love Him and I have *finally* come to know and to trust in Him and His will. I refer to Him often as I write this book. My word for 2020 was Rise… Rise up, Risen-Rise.

As I was researching this word for 2020, I looked up the phrase "rise up" in the scriptures and I was surprised to find how often it appears in the Bible. The phrase "rise up" appears sixty-seven times, "rose up" appears another 104 times and there are many more inexact phrase matches such as "rise ye up," "rise," or "arise" that use the same Hebrew or Greek word translated "rise up."

There are two main Hebrew words translated into "rise up." One is *quwm*, which is translated "to stand up," "to rise up," "to arise," "to raise," "to establish," "to stand," "to perform," "to confirm," "again," "set," "establish," "surely," "continue," "sure," "abide," and "accomplish." It appears in Scripture 629 times and is usually translated by one of the first four translations in this list (498 times combined).

The other word is *shakam*, which means "to rise up early" and that appears sixty-seven times. 'Rise up' must be an important concept in God's eyes. Rise up, to arise, to stand, to continue, to raise up. Rise yourself. It was my word for 2020—Rise, awake, rise up—which as you know, 2020 was quite the opposite of rise. Yet rise, I am continuing to do.

One of my favorite stories in the Bible is after Christ dies, Peter has taken over spreading the Gospel of Jesus Christ and powerfully healing as his Master did.

He comes upon a man in the outer parts of the synagogue, of their church. Here is a man, who has been begging for years and years. He is known by all as one who can't walk. Including by Peter.

Then Peter said, "Silver and gold have I none; but such as I have give I thee: In the name of Jesus Christ of Nazareth RISE UP and walk." (Acts 3:6) [EMPHASIS AUTHOR'S]

And the man does. He rises up with so much joy and walks into the synagogue that so many knew him from the outside.

Watch this—it's beautiful.

He was broken and not able to walk. He was healed by Christ's healing power. He was risen up because of Christ. Because he was risen, we can also rise up. Including those we have buried will rise up again. We are all whole because of Him.

* * *

When we served a mission for our church in Ethiopia quite a few years ago, we taught the people about Jesus Christ. Yet... I questioned how God could possibly know me and know I was there. Ethiopia has billions of people in the country, and millions of people in the large city we lived in—the capital, Addis Ababa.

I remember asking God again and again, "How do you know me and how do you know I am even here?"

I kept asking the members of our church to share with me how they knew God knew them in this plethora of people—millions in one city.

One early morning, I awoke to hear a voice say, "Here I am, RISE UP and be with me."

And I did. I still wake up early and rise up to be with God. He answered my prayers with a, "Rise up and be with me."

There are a number of verses that say, "Rise up early." This is what God has been trying to get me to do for many years now. I never knew how often it was listed in scripture.

As we rise up, we will find and continue to find God loves us infinitely. He knows us, He knows our troubles, our thoughts, our heartaches—He knows all.

* * *

Rising above the death of my baby was the only choice I felt I had. Even when I didn't want to. It might not have been very pretty at times, I probably could have done it better but I rose up. I kept rising up in my life and so can you.

Sometimes it took me until noon or 2:00PM, or even the next day to rise up, but I got up. Time and time again, I continued to rise up.

Rising up is the only way to live this life despite what you're going through. Hope and rising up are not found in the darkness of your room or home. They are found in the light of the world, in God—who is in all of us if we choose to step into that. I know this to be truth.

A sparrow does not fall without Him knowing, including our angels who have gone. He loves you. He knows your heartache. He is there, asking us to rise up with Him. Yet whatever you do, it doesn't matter to Him. He still stays with us. He is unconditional love. No conditions to it.

"For I am sure that neither death nor life, nor angels nor rulers, nor things present nor things to come, nor powers, nor height nor depth, nor anything else in all creation, will be able to separate us from the love of God in Christ Jesus our Lord." (Romans 8:38-39)

If you want to know how to rise above your present circumstances, then consider this: not death, life, angels, rulers, powers, height, depth, things now or yet to come nor anything created can separate you from the love of God in Jesus Christ our Lord. He covers fallen angels and fallen mankind. He covers you and your time of mourning.

As I have said, I believe songs move us beyond the mind and take us directly to the core of our soul.

Music has a powerful way of having us rise up.

Barry Goldstein said about music, "At this deep level we can transmute and transform limited beliefs, negative feelings and emotions."

Music changes and moves me in so many ways. When I'm in a super bad mood or feeling emotional, I can play a powerhouse song and shift my mood or even bring it out with a good needed cry. Listening-crying shifts it.

Crying is good. Crying is bringing it up and out.

I remember in my darkest and hardest times of grief, a song always brought some peace to my soul. It came at exactly the right time and in the right way, speaking light and hope into me. Like Trisha Yearwood's, *The Song Remembers When*.

Has that happened to you?

The song also brought emotions of missing her, intense pain, tender cries and great heartache of questioning why? I just rolled with what was there in the moment.

It's one of the ways I've learned to manage my hopelessness—through the sweet sound of music. Songs spoke to my broken-hearted soul. The words of songs resonated with so many of my emotions.

I believe music is spoken through a special musical spirit. I also believe we learn powerful, spiritual truths through songs and music. I really believe we grow and learn acceptance through songs that touch us.

I so believe we learn to thrive through music. At least in those few minutes it plays.

We are easily moved into tears through music and words in the songs. This, to me, is the Holy Spirit speaking through this amazing gift to us. It can be a way in the beginning of finding healing and the hope we are looking for. Music is a way for us to grow in the learning process we're in. I believe this. Maybe you do, too. I hope you accept this musical concept.

One of our favorite artists at the time of our baby's death was the dynamic Yanni. We'd seen him in concert and loved his beautiful music style.

At our family Christmas party (the final 'normal' Christmas for me), my sister had given us one of Yanni's tapes. Yep, so old it was on a cassette tape.

We played that cassette over and over again. I remember listening to it early Christmas morning, before I found Ariann in her crib, long gone.

There is a song on his album that when I hear it, I am right back in the moment of that morning. It doesn't bring heartache to me. It brings such immense peace. Beautiful Peace. It's difficult to explain.

The song is called *Reflections of Passion*, by Yanni. It's a soulful and heartfelt song. It brings tears to my eyes every time I hear it.

Peaceful tears. Hopeful tears. Sweet tears. Memory tears.

The week after Ariann died, her father and I wanted to get out for a date night. So, we went to a movie. We chose to see Patrick Swayze and Demi Moore in the movie, *Ghost*.

Oh my—what were we thinking? Remember that one? He is killed and she's without him. Then she finds there's someone who can actually hear him. We cried—no bawled—during the whole movie and found such sweet quotes and music throughout it as we began our early healing process.

I can't watch that movie without crying to this day.

The end of the movie immediately brings me to tears, every time. I love it. The light. The beauty. The final moment of realizing it's going to be okay for all.

Sam says to her in the end, "It's amazing, Molly. The love inside you, you take it with you."

Ahhhhhhhhhhhhhhh... You should watch the final scene of the movie *Ghost*.

And then when the ending song plays, and we are in gushing tears again... *Ahhhhhhhh...*

Unchained Melodies *sung by the Righteous Brothers*.

That was probably my first ah-ha moment, after Ari died that music stirred me, opened up the wound, and brought something powerful out in me.

Music has the capacity to assist with the healing process even more quickly, I believe. It's a powerful tool to be able to heal the mind, body, and the soul. It can transform our beings. It touches us where sometimes nothing else can. To be able to blast a song that speaks truth and hope into you, is a game changer—especially in the midst of grief.

Music can help to reverse negative moods, attitudes, and thoughts. It can create powerful actions and inspirations. It's a way to transform us on the deepest level to the core of our being, and change us from the inside out.

Music was a sweet vehicle of how I healed and how I can now heal so quickly from life's trials. Music is a common chord that can knit our hearts as one—creating connection. It's a soul language that speaks to us no matter what we know or feel. Music communicates what words cannot.

One of my favorite moments in my healing journey was receiving a, "thinking of you," message from a friend. It came with a CD that touched my heart with a perfectly timed song for me.

Even as I stayed in my bed for days, I often played music. There would eventually be a song that would have me rise up from hearing it. Still today, it's that way. When I step into the music, it can open up the flood gates.

Have you heard, Vince Gills, *Never Knew Lonely*?

I'll Be Home for Christmas, Where are you, Christmas?.... Really any Christmas song hits me. And Garth Brooks, *The Dance*.

That being said, throughout this book are songs for you that go with the message being shared in each chapter. I encourage you to take a moment to scan the QRCode, crank it up, feel the song in your grieving soul, and journal.

It's a game changer in the process of our learning experiences of life, including in our grief. It's also a way to draw closer to ourselves, to Christ, and to others—especially for those who are in the midst of heartache.

The title of this chapter came from the inspiration from the lyrics of one of my favorite songs, *Rise Up* by Andra Day:

This is definitely a song of hope for all of us. I know it's not easy going on when your heart or mind is not into going on. But as the song says, *"I'll Rise up, despite the ache and I'll do it a thousand times again."* How can you do that?

Rise up?

Do it!

Do that!

Do it with me.

Would you like a rise-up challenge? I ask you to rise up early and see if God is there for you. As you humbly fall to your knees, ask Him if he knows you—if He knows your heartache and knows your pains. Ask Him before you go to bed to wake you up and have you rise up early with Him. Just see if He doesn't answer. I dare you.

"Shake yourself from the dust; arise, sit [on your throne], Jerusalem: loose yourself from the bonds of your neck, captive daughter of Zion." (Isaiah 52:2)

Rise up today. Loose the bonds and rise in Him. Find some music in your day and rise up into your life, despite the loss. Despite where you have been or what has been done to you. Rise up and find some hope in your life. With God. With music.

The questions I would ask you to ask are:

- What was the purpose of this lesson?
- What was the reason I was given this hard?
- Who can I touch today with my experience?
- Whose life needs to be altered through me and my amazing courage?

Rise up for them. Rise up for your angel. Rise up for you.

"Rise up...take courage and do it." (Ezra 10:4)

Rise up and do it a thousand times again. In spite of the ache, the heartache, the loss, the lonely, and the 'I don't feel like it.'

Rise up and do it again and again. For the one you lost.

Journaling Thoughts

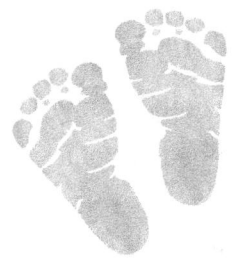

* 9 *

CONNECTION in GRIEVING

"Healing yourself is connected with healing others." ~ Yoko Ono

AHHH, THIS GRIEF JOURNEY. IT'S not where anyone wants to be, and it certainly is not a comfortable place to look in on either. For those of you looking in on us, it's not easy, is it? Just as you can't rush the sunrise to give us morning light, sadly, you also can't rush the growth of the fireweed after the disaster. It grows when it is supposed to grow. But grow it does.

You also can't rush the grief journey.

You can't rush the time of mourning and the steps needing to be taken after losing a loved one or even suffering one of life's hard. It is what it is, when it is, and how it is.

We, in the grief, have to learn to step in to what comes up daily. It is what it is for us. Learning to be with what is for those watching us can be the *real hard* of the journey for you.

The importance of connection with others is crucial.

First let me say…There is *no way* anything you say is going to help or take away the pain. Not a lot of words will even ease it. I *promise*.

As I look back, not anything said to me took away the pain or eased it. Even if there was one thing said to me (or the people's stories I share here) that helped, it wouldn't be the same for others.

The words said to me did not help me. They mostly alienated me and left me feeling even more confused.

What I personally really needed at that hard time was connection—to feel heard and understood, not alone and disconnected.

Connection is feeling a part of, heard, and understood, despite all.

Yet, not much (that I recall) said to me made it easier for me to connect with someone and continue to bear my pain. Some of what was said even left long-time damage in me.

We don't want to do that to another, do we?

I get it. Believe me. I totally get it. We don't know what to say. So we say something we think is comforting or we don't say anything and ignore the grieving souls.

OUCH! That's the hardest one to swallow. I was ignored or turned away from—like I had the plague or something. The *ignore us* choice is such a difficult one for us to navigate—trust me on that. It feels even worse than the crazy statements. Nutty, eh?

Yet, I understand. A few months before my baby died, a couple in our church congregation buried their third son to a rare genetic disease. I was so sad for them. I knew and loved their son, Lucas as we taught him in Sunday school every week. Yet I, not knowing what to say, ignored her completely after he passed. Then, a month later when Ari died, I realized that was harsh to do to her—to not even acknowledge her about losing Lucas, how much I adored him, and how sorry I was.

After Ari's death, I practically ran to her house. I grabbed her and hugged her, saying, "I am so sorry! I didn't know what to say, so I didn't say anything at all. I'm sorry! I am so sad and so sorry for your loss."

It's very simple to say, "I am so sorry for your loss. I can't even imagine." Because trust me, you can't, even if you think you can. You can't.

There is one guarantee in this life—Death—for all of us. Some sooner than later. We are all terminal. That being said, death SUCKS. Trials are hard. No matter who, what, where, when, how—*All of it sucks*. It bites to lose someone earlier than ever anticipated. It really is one of the hardest trials.

To lose someone we love physically hurts. The loss leaves us in a lonely, secluded, and hopeless space. What is said to us or what is not said to us can have a huge impact on us. We already feel like we're the only one dealing with this hard trial, then someone comes along and says something that leaves us feeling reclusive and removed from humanity.

I hope you know what to say. Or maybe you don't. If you've ever lost someone close to you—real close to you, then you know.

It's hard losing someone in this life. Yet, after their death you become part of an exclusive club you didn't even know existed. The MY BABY DIED club. The MY CHILD DIED club. The MY MOM DIED club. The MY SPOUSE DIED club. The MY DAD DIED club, or even The MY GRANDPARENTS WHOM I LOVED DEARLY DIED club, and so on.

It really doesn't matter their age, their health, their life, or anything—we grieve because we loved, and we lost them. It's one of the hards of life.

From the funeral, to the out-of-town guests, to the food, to so much more to worry about—You *do not* anticipate one of the worst parts is going to be *other people* and what they say to you or about you during this time.

I know it's not all of us. I know I didn't know what to say or do either. I feel there are many of us not knowing how to be comfortable in the face of death and people's grief. Even me standing there crying after my baby died was so uncomfortable for people. They couldn't be with or around me and my big sadness.

"Please don't cry. It's okay—she's in a good place." That one is said *way* too much. And we don't want to hear it.

I know death is uncomfortable. I am living in it. Discomfort, and all.

As I look back at the time after the funeral, the actions that mattered to me came from the heart of others—The food that showed up. Neighbors who came in to help us move or clean our home. Friends who spent time with me in silence, letting me cry. Cards that came in the mail from people I didn't even know with, "I'm so sorry for your loss," or "You are in our thoughts and prayers," and money.

All the money that poured in from people all around to assist us with the cost of the funeral immensely touched us. We were able to pay for her funeral and headstone and take a week off work with the money given to us by so many touching souls.

There are many do-gooders out there, I know there are. I had numerous show up to give of themselves whom I might not have acknowledged. I am sorry if that outpouring of kindness didn't happen with anybody else and their experience. It needs to always be that way.

Can I just take a moment and publicly THANK ALL of you who did do so much for us at that most devastating time in our lives? Words are all I have right now, but one day I hope to hug you all and say, "Thank you. Thank you. Thank you."

Thank you for those who showed up so beautifully for us.

My mom said, "It takes a village to raise a child and I also know it takes a village to bury a child." I know this, too, and I am so, so grateful. A village of loving, connecting souls is what every death is in need of.

Don't we all want to be that for someone who has lost?

There are touching ways we can make a difference for someone who is grieving. I hope we can all step into what that looks like, so we can *master the art of connection* in the time of grief. It's a gift to have. It's a gift worth developing.

For me, the real hard stuff—the words said—started at the funeral. Words that triggered the pain, the heartache, the guilt, the hurt, all the crappy stuff. The triggers around the death. The words spoken, not in any intentionally mean way or wanting to cause pain way, I hope, but yet they did.

I want to believe people were trying to be comforting and helpful, but their words *so* didn't help. Looking back, even some of the crazier statements *really* felt so hurtful. They cut like a dagger into my heart. So many of the words spoken at the funeral by people coming to mourn did not bring peace to me. More just triggered my heartache, my *Mom Guilt*, and some even made me angrier—which I was a lot back then.

"She was too perfect for this life."

"You must be so strong to handle this one."

"She's in God's arms now."

"She's in a better place."

"Time will heal this wound."

"I know exactly how you feel."

"You will get over this."

"This, too, shall pass."

"You're young. You can have another one."

"Good thing you still have your husband."

People relating stories of *their* or *other's* hards—did *not* help me at all in that time. I know this sounds harsh, but it felt harsh.

I stood there, two days after Christmas, by the tiniest casket of my first-born baby girl—preparing to bury her little body forever. What was being said didn't help me step into connecting or finding any peace around what I was personally going through.

It was about my pain and heartache needing to be justified and feeling like it was not okay where I was at in that heartbreaking moment.

By the time the funeral services were over, I was in shock. I felt so completely alone. I felt like no one had connected with or even had felt me—my intense loss and screaming grief. They didn't understand. I felt like a complete loner—one who wanted all of it to pass. One who didn't deserve Ari. One who did *not* understand her own strength, who didn't get why God was holding Ari instead of her.

Why was that a better place for my Ari? How the fricken heck can time heal this wound? How could anyone know exactly how I feel? How am I going to go on from this?

That began my biggest frustration with my loss journey—people not knowing what to say to 'deal' with it and me.

I am not alone in what I am saying. I've interviewed hundreds of people who have lost big. I have found similar stories and heart-breaking scenarios that hit hard for them, too.

We lived in a small town in southern Utah, so we were well known as the parents of the baby who had died of SIDS. There were a few people who really showed up for me at that broken time.

There were also so many people who did not show up to connect with me at that time, or who showed up with their inappropriate comments—which were spoken as if the words were truth and even okay to say.

I'll share with you the one that hit me the hardest. The one I held on to the longest and simply made no sense to me as to why someone would say it.

A *few* months after Ariann's death, a lady came into my job and actually said, "Oh, you're the one who buried her baby? Can I ask you, did you breast feed?"

"No," I said. "I tried so hard, and it wasn't working for me or her and I finally had to feed her formula."

"Oh," she said. "One of the studies we've been doing here at Dixie State says babies who are not breast fed are ninety-eight percent more likely to die of SIDS."

What the ?!?

Who *seriously* says that to someone after the loss of their child? It doesn't matter if you have a study that is a hundred percent guaranteed—is that appropriate to say to a grieving mom?

How stupid and hurtful to say. Seriously? 'Here's your sign!' (I will explain that later) Not nice at all. I don't care if it's true, which I don't believe it is, *now*. But, I did for a long time.

Even if it is truth, does it need to be said? We are dealing with a huge loss. Are studies or statistics or your way of thinking or telling me any of your 'truth' going to help me bear my burden? Is it going to connect with me?

I had enough of my own *Mom Guilt* (as do others going through their own grief), I didn't need extra stuff added on top of it.

We don't need the useless *should've/could've/why didn't yous* added to the stuff we're already carrying.

The interesting part about being a mom and losing a child is there is so much *Mom Guilt* we place upon ourselves. Really the harshest things being said are being said by ourselves to ourself. It's a very sad part of burying a child—or burying any loved one, really. We *should* on ourselves way too much, anyway. Add a death/trial and we really *should've* on ourselves.

I should have been there...

I should have been home...

I should not have gone back to work...

I should have checked on her earlier...

I should have not put her in that blanket, in that nightgown, in that hot room...

I should not have let her go...

I should/should not have vaccinated her....

I should have spent more time with them...

I should have said... or done...

Should've/Could've/Would've changed...

Why didn't I do this or do that...

What if this?

What if that?

What if?

As I was reading through my journal after her death, I came upon a whole page of me asking these questions:

> *Why would God take something so special from me? Why me? Why this? What could I have done? Was God punishing me for what I did in my past? Was I to blame because I did not breast feed?*

Did she cry and I didn't hear her? Was I a bad mom? What did I miss? What could I have done differently? Why did I go back to work and take her to daycare? Why didn't I get her checked out again when she wasn't feeling good?

Why did she go? What could I have done differently? Why her? Why me? Why? Why? Why?

How do I go on? How do I survive this? How do I move forward? Why would I want to move forward? Why do my arms ache so bad? Why do I hear her crying in the night and I cannot seem to get to her? Why was it this way?

Why had God betrayed me in such a heartbroken way?

I was screaming to myself with *so* many questions running through the depths of my darkest grief and pain. I was screaming, "WHY? WHY? WHY?"

No one seemed to hear me. There were no answers to be found in the darkness of that void.

Thank goodness this is normal. Or is this normal? What is normal? I am not sure, but I think whatever we are feeling in grief is normal.

You see, even after her death, I had my own stuff I was putting on myself. I didn't need what was being said to me to add to my huge pile of stuff.

Sadly, I believed some of those words at the time. Yep—I believed them and carried them around with me for a very long time.

One of the posts I found in my journal before she died said this,

For the past week or so, you had been on an, "I want my mommy kick," crying anytime I put you down.

> *It felt good and I loved to be needed by you, but this week being Christmas, I needed to get things done so, I laid you on the blanket by me and I let you cry.*

Dang *Mom Guilt*. There's a lot of *Mom Guilt* around a death of a child. Well—let's be truthful, there is just plan and simply a lot of *Mom Guilt* we carry in life with all our babies, living or dead.

> *It's me crying now. Why didn't I just hold you? Why didn't I hold tight to you?*

Those words, the breastfeeding one being my fault words, were one of the harshest conversations that I felt punched me in the gut. Because I actually believed it for a long time—that I *should have* pushed breastfeeding more on her. I *should have* tried harder at it. It just didn't work for me or her.

One of the phrases said to me a lot, was, "She was just so special."

I remember thinking, *Why did I have to have a special one? Why couldn't she stay and still be special? Why?*

Here's the thing—we don't know *how* to go on or *how* to survive this or *how* to move forward.

Yet, it feels like people think they know how for us.

They do not.

Here's another thing—we are *not* going to get over it. '*Time to move on*' isn't what needs to be said.

Having another baby is not going to help. I tried that.

So, maybe those 'words of misplaced wisdom' don't need to be stated…

Stay tuned for what can be said to connect with us in this hard time.

Lauren Dagle, You Say

I love that song… It took me a long time to be solid in that what others said to me or about me or my life was none of their or my business—not my circus, not my monkeys.

Not mine to take on. The only thing that matters to me now is what He says about me.

Journaling Thoughts

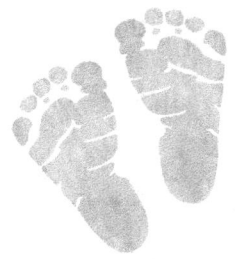

* 10 *

HERE's your SIGN

"Somethings are better left unsaid, which I generally realize right after I have said them." ~ *Crazy Momma*

THE FUNNY COMEDIAN, BILL ENGVALL has a "Here's your sign" series of jokes that are really quite funny. His concepts are simply about saying something that is... not smart at all. Even if we know it's not smart, we still say it. It's quite funny how he presents it.

We all have that tendency in us. It's really about being mindful of what we say.

I sometimes felt like having one or two of those signs handy to hang around the neck of people who said *The Stupid Things* was necessary. Insensitive words are some of the most difficult hurts for those of us who just lost big in our lives and are easily triggered.

Hearing words that are not only hurtful but also incredibly inane is sometimes the most difficult part of the grief journey.

Sorry if that sounds harsh, but let's keep talking about what that looks like so we all see what I mean. Even more than what it looks like, how about how it feels for those on the other end of the words being said.

This is true for everything.

[Lately, watching social media I am seriously appalled.]

There are words to say and words not to say at this time. Why say hurtful things which leave us feeling disconnected from you and others, instead of helpful words. I write with the hope I can enlighten you in what absolutely not to say, while giving you some pointers in what works to say at the time of death, grief, and heartache times in people's lives.

Let's talk about what we *are* saying at the time of hardship or after deaths. Sadly, it's not very good.

As I have been researching this book for many years, I heard things said and cringed—the added heartache and pain it caused the people who were grieving their losses. I know we are ultra-sensitive at this open-wounded time. But there are some things we just don't want to hear anymore.

Do I still have you with me? Do you know what I am talking about? I am hoping you step in to this and really want to learn what to say or do for someone in great loss.

"A gentle answer turns away rage, but a hash word stirs up anger." (Proverbs 15:1)

The tongue has no bones but is truly strong enough to break a heart. We must be careful with our words and what we say, especially during life's hards.

As the scriptures says, "there is...a time to be silent, and a time to speak." (Ecclesiastes 3:7)

There are a dozen or more people on our grief-journey road who have *no idea* what to say. They can't even be around us in this time.

The even sadder part is they say *crazy* stuff—even hurtful stuff that doesn't need to be said—words that leave us triggered and pushing away from them, not being able to add them into our safe circle of people who grieve with us.

They will not be the ones we turn to in our deepest, darkest, and loneliest hours.

In our grief, *they* will be the ones we tell our safe-space people about and what *they* said to us that didn't make any sense in finding healing and peace.

We are looking for those who can be open, accepting, and heartfelt for us. We're looking for connection. We're looking for those who step into us and let us find a safe space to heal in them. Those are the people we're looking for.

My advice, keep reading. Don't get handed an *Engvall sign*. Educate yourself in what is appropriate to say. Learn from this book on what is going to create connection and help facilitate healing for someone you care about who is grieving.

Also, for those of you who are grieving, in the feeling of your own loss do not let stupid statements trigger you. Do not hold on to the harsh words, like I did.

I really took their words to heart and believed them—even getting mad at times. I believed in the truth of some and let them affect me for a very long time. Way too long.

Looking back, I should've said, "Thanks for sharing and no thanks for that—not taking that on."

I really wish I would've offered more grace and more compassion to those who were uncomfortable around my grief. But I was young and triggered. I had not done much personal development to realize it was their stuff and their pain coming out.

It was so *not* mine to take on. All part of their and my lesson. All part of the learning into the growth of this life.

Let's see if we can't educate us all.

* * *

"I don't always put my foot in my mouth, sometimes I get both of them in."

Say What?

We've probably all heard someone say, "Did you just put your foot in your mouth?," or "Shoot, I just put my foot in my mouth." It happens to the best of us.

To 'put your foot in your mouth' is to say something you should not have said, especially something that embarrasses or hurts someone else.

We all say things we regret. If you're anything like me, you also put your 'foot in your mouth' on regular occasions. If you *are* anything like me, then I know you're a caring and loving person and YOU do not intentionally look for ways of hurting people.

At least I hope not.

I especially did not know what to say or do at the uncomfortable time of death and grieving. Most don't. Unless you've really been through it in some way, you won't know.

Maybe we don't know what we're saying is hurtful or not even helpful. Maybe we're too uncomfortable around death, grief, and mourning. Maybe we just don't know what to say. I get it. You could be like me—sometimes thoughts just pop into my head and then they jump, feet-first out my mouth. This could be your excuse, too, and the sole reason for saying something not so appropriate.

You just don't know what to say, so you say the first thought that pops out your mouth.

Deanna Wadsworth is credited for having said there are "...[f]our things you can't recover: The stone after the throw, The word after it's said, The occasion after it's missed, The time after it's gone."

After the death of my baby and during the raw time of my mourning, I heard many things that were so hard to hear. Besides the crazy breast-feeding one, there were many more which left me feeling isolated, alone, and confused.

You have to remember, grievers are not in normal, able-to-roll-it-off-their-backs, easy spaces. We are experiencing the hardest, most difficult time of our life. Our minds are so not *okay* at this time *and* we are already negative-talking to ourselves.

When I first thought about writing this book, I thought of naming it, 1000 STUPID THINGS PEOPLE SAY (at the time of death). It was a crazy list of things people said that left such hurt, disconnect, and even somewhat damaging to me, or so I felt. I was not in the space of hearing even half of what was being said, anyway. I already felt damaged, broken, disconnected from everyone and the words being said created more brokenness, more disconnect, and even more loneliness.

As you can see, God inspired me with the title and gave me the space to say it with love. We all have that in us.

Joel Osteen said, "Be Careful of what you say. You can say something hurtful in ten seconds, but ten years later, the wounds are still there."

It is so true. Thirty years later, I still remember the hurtful words said during that tender time for me.

You will see, some of these are said in times of loss all of the time. Some are said some of the time. Some are just crazy should-not-have-ever-been said, but still said.

"Here's your sign."

There are definitely worst things said, but the list I provide are ones that are not okay to say at all, really.

One of the horrible statements I heard was, "At least she wasn't eighteen and had her whole life a head of her."

What the ??? WHY? Does anyone truly believe this to be truth? Because it so is *not*! No, she wasn't eighteen. She was four months old *and* she still had a whole life a head of her. Remember, it doesn't matter their age, their health, their lifestyle or anything else—all that matters to us is that they are gone and they really meant something so deeply to us. They were OUR future no matter what age or illness or anything else.

Here is the thing about 'At least'…

Saying 'at least' is not a way to start creating connection with us. It's not a way of starting to comfort us. It immediately creates disconnect. 'At least' is *never* a start to saying something to ease or assist with our pain. 'At least' is NOT an appropriate way to try and comfort us.

"At least, she didn't suffer…"

"At least, you had four months…."

"At least, they are out of pain…"

"At least, you got to say goodbye to them…"

"At least, you have another one…"

"At least, you can get remarried…"

"At least they went quickly…"

"At least she is with God…"

"At least…"

At least—At least—At least…

Don't ever start a sentence to comfort someone with AT LEAST. At least, 'here's your sign.' At least, you aren't our safe space. At least, I can unfriend you and never see you again, or try my best not to ever see you again. At least, you are not my tribe. At least, you might grieve yourself someday. At least... *Ahhhhh*—'Bless your heart,' said as the Southerners say.

Once again, nothing you say is going to make this better or heal this for us. Someone is handling incredible pain and heartache and you're thinking you're going to sugar-coat it, silver-line it, or try and make it better. It's not possible. So don't try. I repeat, do not *ever* start with AT LEAST... At least, we can move on from this 'at least'. Thank goodness.

The next horrible comment to me really blew me away. "Good thing you all are young, you can have another one." (This might be true yet, it does not make it better for us.) Yes, we know we are young and we can have another one, but right now we're sad and grieving *this one* we loved.

Your words do not make the grief easier, better nor are they even right to say. Another one would be *another* one. But not *this* one. Not our Ariann Maree. Not the hope of *this* one. Do you get what I am saying?

'Good thing' is another inappropriate start of comforting us.

"Good thing no more pain."

"Good thing she's in God's hand now."

"Good thing she is saved."

"Good thing you will get over this."

Someone at the time of my little sister's death said to my older sister, "Good thing you have like ten other brothers and sisters."

What the ????

'Good thing' is *not* the start of comfort at this time.

"Here's your sign."

This one is said...*way too much.*

"She was just too perfect for this world," or "She was just such a perfect, special soul who did not need this earth experience."

Hearing how perfect she was just infuriated me and made me wish I would've had a non-perfect or not special child like most people.

"Maybe she was too perfect."

I know she was. Yet, I don't care to hear this one, either. She was too perfect for me, or so I already thought. Lots of babies and kids and even people are too perfect for this world and yet they get to stay. This one does not make it easier for us. She could still be perfect and still be in my arms. I know others who have 'perfect' babies and kids who don't die, so why mine?

Can we please retire that one?

Someone said, "It's part of God's plan."

This one was said to me and to other people I interviewed so many times. A lot of the people I spoke with, all had the solid foundation of the gospel of Jesus Christ in their life. That was not the issue. Yet hearing this said to them did not bring comfort or ease to their pain. Even in the midst of knowing what you know, you still don't want to be told what you know. Because sometimes that brings up emotions in knowing that "God's plan" took a precious life from you. Just for that moment, it's not something we want told to us.

C.S. Lewis said when people told him he should be happy because his wife was now in God's hands and this was His plan, he said he didn't agree. He thought she was in God's hands when she was alive, and look at how she suffered with a horrible disease.

Some people say suffering is part of God's agenda, but helping someone who is grieving is a matter of compassion and connection, not theology or what God's plan is.

We can't explain God's plan or His hands so maybe we shouldn't even try during a time of grief. Let the grief-stricken figure out if that's true.

Which is what I had to do for myself. I had to come to the testimony and my own *ah-ha* moment that it was part of God's plan. (Way more to come on this.) Now, if and when we say it ourselves, we are finally feeling able to feel the ease of the death.

Not during the midst of it.

You can't explain that to all people. It doesn't bring comfort to those who don't even believe in God's plan or are not okay with God's plan at the time. I don't think it's the moment to try and share His plan with them. There might be a time for that later, if you can step into their safe space by not saying something hurtful, triggering, or upsetting to them.

Even standing in her strong foundation of the gospel of Jesus Christ, saying this to my mom did not ease or comfort her at her grieving time.

One of my mom's least favorite ones said to her was, "She's in a better place."

My mom really disliked hearing this after it was said to her so many times. *The better place* was in her arms, and she responded with that.

She *knows* God's plan. God's plan is *awesome*. It is a beautiful plan. We can look back at *life's hards* and maybe say, "Oh yes, I get why."

During the trial—in that moment, you don't *get why* you're hurting, begging for a different plan, asking God to take the hurt from you.

Just as Jesus Christ did in the Garden of Gethsemane, "Lord remove this cup from me." (Luke 22:42)

In the moments of our grief, our *hards*, God's plan may have an adverse reaction for us. Sadly, it is not uplifting to hear when we are dealing with our own Gethsemane moments.

Let's talk about some more 'unmentionables' I want to share with you. Are you ready for them? Here is a list of some of the comments said (not all to me) which are *not* appropriate to say to anyone at any time of grief:

- She lived a long enough life in this life.
- He/she is in a better place.
- She/he brought this on themselves.
- Time heals all wounds.
- Buck up, this is part of life.
- You have your husband, hold on to him [said to me after Ariann's death].
- There is a reason for everything.
- Don't hold on to this one, let it go.
- Aren't you over it yet? It's been a while.
- You can have another child.
- Good thing you have another baby [twin died].
- Thank goodness for your other kids.
- God must have known you could handle this. You are so strong to have God trust you with this.
- She was such a good person, God wanted her with Him.
- I know exactly how you feel.
- Your mom is helping you all to be so independent, she was preparing you [her mom died when she was eight years old].

- She did what she came here to do and it was her time to go.
- You've got this handled!
- People have been through worse.
- Death of a parent is easier than them divorcing.
- At least you only lost one.
- Well, everyone dies.
- Was he saved?! Hope he makes it to Heaven.
- What you are doing/going through is not normal.
- We are all just hoping you can snap out of this soon.
- Must have been her time to go.
- It's been long enough, move on.
- God needed her more than you.
- They are at peace. You should be, too.
- Too bad she didn't take better care of herself.
- What did he die from?
- Aren't you mad at him for not taking care of himself?
- What happened? I've been looking for information but can't find any.
- They died doing what they loved.
- Awwwww, life is so rough. Let me tell you what I am going through.
- Better widowed than divorced.
- Oh good, you have moved on.
- God needed another rose for His garden.
- This, too, shall pass.
- Is her house going on the market soon? [We recently got this one all the time with the passing of my husband's mom.]

A Time to Mourn

- Why is it a closed casket?
- I understand what you are going through.
- Your are so strong to be able to go through this.
- Don't cry. They wouldn't want you to be sad.
- Trust in God's plan and His way.
- You are so cold around this death [said to me when my pampa died].
- It's time to get on with your life—have another one/get remarried, get over it!
- What was he/she thinking?! [Said to my friend after her son was killed in a car high-jacking/drug deal.]
- That wasn't too smart of him/her/them.
- This, too, shall pass, hopefully very quickly.
- They wouldn't want to see you like this.
- They can't Rest In Peace until you move on.
- She was old and ready to go.
- Trust in God's timing.
- Been there, done that.
- Do you think they regret what they did now?
- I get exactly what you are feeling.
- At least you aren't going through what so-and-so is going through.
- Time to let them go. Move on.
- When are you selling her stuff/cleaning out her closet? [This was one my mom dealt with a lot.]
- Time to smile.
- No one wants you living like this.
- Fake it until you can make it.

- Focus on the good and the future ahead of you.
- Time to clean out and get rid of their stuff. They don't need it. [Never is it time until it is.]
- Are you going to create a lawsuit around their death?
- Are you going to charge the person involved in this?
- You're sad. How can we get you over that?

One of the *worst things* to do is *to not say anything*—just ignore me.

- Asking 'How are you?' within the year of their death is not appropriate. My husband went through this one recently when he lost his mom to cancer in April 2020. Everyone kept asking, "How are you?"

He wasn't good. But what do you say when it's constantly asked of you, "How are you?"

"Fine," or "I'm okay" is going to be your answer. But we aren't okay. We aren't fine. We are sad, grieving, and feeling the pain of loss.

- I thought you'd be over it by now.
- Now, she will never go to heaven. Why did the family burn her spirit? [After hearing loved one was cremated.]
- It's not a big deal because, literally everyone dies.
- Get over it.
- I'll call you, check in on you, and we can get together. [But then never called.]
- It's kind of like you got divorced.
- I hear that's the worst way to die.
- If my child died, I would be happy because I would know he is in Heaven.

- You have to be strong.
- Now you can live your own life rather than taking care of a disabled child.
- *Nothing.* [Made no acknowledgment.]
- What did he go and do now?
- Don't be depressed. No one likes people who are depressed.
- You've lost so many people, it probably doesn't even phase you anymore.
- My phone rang and it was a church *friend*. She asked me what was wrong, I told her my mother had just passed away a few hours before and she said, "Oh, don't let anyone go through her house until I get there. I want to see what she had." [A friend's share.]
- You should be rejoicing.
- At least he made it to ninety-two.
- Look on the bright side.
- We all have problems.
- When telling someone how I believe seeing cardinals is a sign: "That's not theologically possible." [A friend's share.]
- What did you think was going to happen? He was a drug addict.
- Well, you know your father *will* marry again [weeks after a friend's mom died].
- That's life!
- You've lost all your joy.
- Everything happens for a reason.
- You need to stop feeling sorry for yourself and move on.
- Your sad dreams and nightmares aren't normal.
- Wow, they're dropping like flies [on hearing of a husband's death].
- You're too young to know what real grief is.

- I forgive you for being such a B!@tch. I know you're grieving.
- God never gives you more than you can handle.
- Just put it back in the drawer, it doesn't belong here [in reference to a friend sharing a memory of her mum].
- I don't want to sound mean, but you need to move forward. She's not coming back.
- Don't be sad when there's so much to be grateful for.
- God needed him more than you do.
- Well, you're the man of the house now [said to a twelve-year-old son].
- I am going to hang up now—call me back when you stop crying.
- Everyone's just waiting for you to snap.

After our twenty-year-old daughter died in a traffic accident, a lady said she knew how we felt because their dog had died the week before.

- This is a day for celebration! [at my mom's memorial service].
- If I went through everything you did, I'd have killed myself.
- That's why you shouldn't have had a lot of kids.
- That's why you should have had a lot of kids.
- Remember, others have it worse than you.
- At least you're young, you can have another.
- You really should snap out of it! People die.
- Imagine Christmas in Heaven for her [my baby].
- He's floating around in "purgatory" [my loved one who wasn't baptized].
- You can enter the room again when you stop crying.
- You're being selfish.

- I can't imagine what it was like for your mum when she died.
- It was her time.
- Even this will pass.
- Life should be more than just grief—let it go.
- Too bad he killed himself. He's a lost soul now.
- Losing your husband is nothing compared to a parent, you can replace a husband.

*　*　*

Oh my gosh. Can you believe some of those? All of them, really. Yes, those really were said to me and other people in their time of grief. I know there are so many more and I know by writing this I will hear even more.

Can you believe these were said to people in their deepest mourning moments? Some are definitely worse than others but either way these are not words to say to anyone, let alone grieving souls. The comments said are trying to correct their grief, trying to take it away with callous and insensitivities that are not going to leave anyone feeling heard, connected with, or loved on.

We most likely will not turn to someone who says any of this stuff in our greatest time of need. We will also probably talk to people we trust about these words being said to us, and you don't want that, right?

There's a notion of, "Move on already, get over it, stop feeling it, it's done, have another baby, get another husband."

It kind of feels like people are saying to us, "Yeah, just deal with this and don't get in my way as you deal with it."

There's such an attitude of, "Aren't you over this yet?"

That's certainly not how *we* want to come across to anyone in the deep abyss of their grief, is it? We just don't know what to say, do we?

I get it, believe me. Remember Lucas' mom from a past chapter? Grief is so uncomfortable. It's not just uncomfortable for those going through it. It's uncomfortable for those who are around it, looking in at it.

Watching us, you want us to quickly get through it. It seems to be really uncomfortable for those who are looking in—looking at us going through it, wondering, "What do I do or say?"

I wrote this book for all of us to create a space—a clear space for those of us grieving to just *be* in, no matter what stage of grief we're in. That's my hope. A clear, open, beautiful, loving, accepting-with-open-arms-ready-to-love-us-through-this space.

Are you willing to do it? Are you willing to walk in that space for some time so you can be part of someone's healing tribe? Are you willing to show up that way for us? Are you willing to get uncomfortable with us?

We need the ones who are *in* with us.

I realize you might not *get it* right now. Until you step into it yourself. Then, when you're the one sitting in the front row at the funeral, saying, "Oh!" Then you *get it*. Until then, you won't truly understand.

Yet, we want you to get it. We want you to have empathy for us and for others, and to step into our grieving shoes, as uncomfortable as that is. We're asking all (or some) to get over the uncomfortable and find comfort in consoling those of us who are on our grief roller-coaster ride.

To be able to ask, "What is it like for those sitting in the front row after losing a child, a husband, parents, or someone so dear to them, tragically, unexpectedly or slowly, painfully? What is that like? How does that feel? What would I want to hear from them or have them to do to support me in my grief journey?"

A TIME TO MOURN

Until you can truly know their journey, you don't *get it*. At one point, you're going to be looking at me and my grief and say, "I don't get it."

You don't understand. And then one day you will say, "Now, I get it."

Then, we will be there for you in a way you will appreciate. We will have empathy for you. We will then be that open, loving, accepting-with-open-arms-ready-to-love-you-through-this-space tribe. Only because we get it. We have felt it, somewhat, and we know what to do and say, and we definitely know what *not* to say. But we know and we got you.

We'll be that for you. Can you learn to be that for us?

There is a song we sang in church when I was a young girl called *Kindness Begins With Me* and it says, "I want to be kind to everyone, for that is right, you see. So I say to myself, 'Remember this: Kindness begins with me.'"

Remember the words you speak are either *kind* or *not kind*, even as you speak to those in mourning. Ask yourself, "Would I want this said to me? Is it necessary? Is it kind? Does it really need to be said to them?"

Clear, loving and thoughtful is kind.

IN A WORLD WHERE YOU CAN BE ANYTHING, BE KIND.

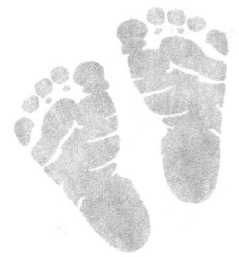

* 11 *

SYMPATHY VS. EMPATHY

"Empathy fuels connection. Sympathy drives disconnection." ~ Dr. Brené Brown

I TRULY BELIEVE BRENÉ BROWN HAD been Divinely guided in some of her work. She wrote so much about empathy and connection as a researcher. She worked on changing the game of life with hitting it head on, sharing about vulnerability, connection, and what that looked like.

Vulnerability, connection, and empathy are game changers in the grief journey.

Oh—this is where my husband says we are going to talk about the 'F' word...Feelings. He makes me laugh. When I ask him about something or about someone, he says, "That's a girl question," and "Are we talking about the 'F' word right now?"

Feelings. Well, let's talk about feelings and even think about asking some 'girl' questions. Okay?

The interesting thing about death, loss, pain, and grief is that communication and connection—sympathy vs empathy—are so very complicated during times of grief. What might have been comforting for someone else to hear, could be something that triggers me or leaves me feeling dishonored in my grief.

A friend told me one of her sweetest memories after her baby died was when a neighbor lady showed up with two children and a baby. The lady let my friend hold the baby, as the lady knew my friend's arms would be aching.

That would *not* have worked for me. Most days after, I felt resentful toward others who still had their babies. A friend of mine named her baby Ariann just like mine, and she still had her Ariann with her. I did not. I felt anger around that, and other babies being around me early on.

The emotional roller-coaster grief ride never looks the same for anyone. We need to listen to our inner knowing, our intuition, and the Holy Spirit telling us how we approach each person. It's going to need to be guided and lighted by the Spirit for us to help someone on their grief road. We might just need to get into their home and really ask the 'girl' questions, or just be there with them and for them.

Remember, no two losses are the same. No two people want the same in their time of grieving. Listening to what to do, to be guided to reach out and hear what they need from us. Asking the girl questions—the feeling questions with meaning. Learn what really needs to happen for them.

We don't ask the questions for us or for our own knowledge, it's important we ask the questions to take care and love on them.

After my friend's wife was diagnosed with Stage-IV cancer and people asked him questions about it, he asked them, "Are you just curious or do you really care?"

As we look at the words we say, we might want to ask ourselves that question.

"Am I curious or do I really care?"

Looking back through the list, there are not many caring statements.

Curious?—Yes!

Inappropriate?—Yes!

Mean?—Yes!

Hurtful?—Yes!

Caring?—Not so much.

In talking about sympathy vs. empathy, there are words we say that stem from being sympathetic. There are things we say that come from being empathetic. You're probably asking what the difference between the two is.

There's a huge difference.

Let me give you the definitions and give you some further explanation for you to understand the difference in the two words.

sym·pa·thy

/ˈsimpəTHē/

noun feelings of pity and sorrow for someone else's misfortune. "They had great sympathy for the fire victims."

Commiseration, pity, condolence, consolation…

Do those words sound like connection to you? Not really, right?

em·pa·thy

/ˈempəTHē/

noun the ability to understand and share the feelings of another. The term "empathy" is used to describe a wide range of experiences.

Emotion researchers generally define empathy as the ability to sense other people's emotions, coupled with the ability to try to imagine what someone else might be thinking or feeling. To have affinity with, rapport with, sympathy with, understanding of, sensitivity toward, sensibility to, identification with, awareness of, fellowship with, fellow feeling for, like-mindedness, togetherness, closeness to.

To me, empathy sounds like connection and sympathy sounds like disconnection. Maybe?

Connection is defined as: A relationship in which a person or thing is linked or associated with something else. The action of linking one thing with another. Other words are bond, relatedness, and connectedness.

The difference between the most commonly used meanings of these two terms sympathy and empathy is: Sympathy is feeling sorry or sorrow, or pity for the hardships another person encounters. Empathy is feeling with the other person and putting yourself in their shoes. Really being able to be with them while they are feeling in their grief—this is empathy.

Rebecca O'Donnell is quoted as having said, "Empathy is walking a mile in somebody else's shoes. Sympathy is being sorry their feet hurt after their mile walk."

One creates connection and one creates disconnection. You can tell when someone is feeling sorry for you (sympathy) or feeling with you (empathy).

Can't *you*? I sure feel it.

Can you see how different those two words are? Connection or disconnection—which one do you want to create with another person? Which one do you want to be known for? One who brings connection in, or not?

Me personally, I want to connect and be connected to, especially in grueling times of mourning and hard stuff in life.

Brené Brown defined connection as, "The energy that exists between people when they feel seen, heard, and valued, when they can give and receive without judgment, and when they derive sustenance and strength from the relationship."

Sympathy is saying, "I know how you feel."

Do we *really* know how they feel? Do we know how anyone truly feels? *I* don't think so. Because, really, can we *ever* really know how someone feels? It's their shoes they're standing in and we'll never know what that's like. Never.

Saying, "I know how you're feeling," does not create connection. It creates disconnection. It was *one* of the biggest disconnects for me, when someone said, "I know how you're feeling."

Really, *you* know how *I* am feeling? Did you wake up Christmas morning and the baby you bore and loved so much had died during the night? *Your* first born died on Christmas Day, too? You know how I feel? Have *you* ever wanted to end your life? Have you really felt my pain, my guilt, my grief? Are you walking in *my* sad shoes?

Sadly, no—you can never, ever, know how anyone feels in their time of great loss. No one felt what I felt. I did not feel what Ari's dad felt. I did not feel what my mom felt. I do not know what you're feeling. I can't know what your grief journey is like. Even if anyone thinks they have experienced the exact same loss, it's never ever going to be the same experience.

Empathy is the ability to step into the shoes of another person, aiming to understand *their* feelings and perspectives, to then use that understanding to guide your actions to do good. Feeling with me means be with me. Sit with me. Even in silence, if necessary. Finding a way to connect with me even in my grief. Say words to connect with me. Find ways of being with me, around me, and serving me to have me step in to connecting with you in my time of mourning.

One of the most difficult statements for someone in grief to hear is, "I'm here for you if you need anything."

Here's the thing—we don't know what we need, let alone who to call for it. Do you really want to make a difference for someone in their grief? Show up at their home, invite/push yourself in and start doing what needs to be done, even if that means sitting with them on the couch and crying with them.

Saying to them, "I am coming over Tuesday to bring you a meal and to help with your laundry." Or, "I have time on Thursday to run some errands for you. What can I do?" Or, "I am coming on Sunday to be with you."

Sometimes we just have to show up in their world to illustrate we're there for them. You know the saying, "Actions speak louder than words." Let's *act*.

Why don't we start asking ourselves some key questions?

"Am I trying to relieve their pain in some way?"

"Is what I am saying necessary to say?"

"If I say this, is it going to create connection or disconnection?"

"Am I curious or do I really care?"

There are many ways of creating connection in the time of death and heartache.

Saying, "I am so sorry. I can't even imagine what you are going through," is *so* great.

It's a simple phrase and yet it creates a sense of, "I feel you but I don't know what or how you are feeling," "I am so sad for you and your family," "You are in my many thoughts and prayers," (Mean it and go pray for them), "I am so sorry—what can I do for you?"

Even saying, "I am coming over on this day, be ready for me to bring you food/to clean/to run errands/to watch your kids while you do anything you need to do or nothing at all."

That's being there. That's how we create connection. The gift of being empathetic with someone in grief is a game-changer and will assist them in finding peace. It will leave them feeling as if they are understood and heard, even in their craziest moments.

Empathy means, "I'm in this with you, I'm here for you, to feel this with you, to let you know that you are not alone."

Empathetic means you aren't trying to change it, fix it, or make it right or better. That cannot be done.

What can we do instead for them? Who can we be for them? How could we show up differently for them? You know, if we really want to make a difference for someone in that moment, wondering what we could do, instead of thinking of something we can say. *Nothing* we say will make it better or even comfort them.

No one should expect us to have the words that will erase their pain. We can't undo their loss—which is the only thing that could make it better or even bearable right at the moment. Nothing can fix it, so we *all* have to learn to be with it, including those looking in.

Your presence can help them bear the pressing weight of their grief. *If* you are completely empathetic. No judgments, no other way of being—just being there for them.

> *Empathy is a strange and powerful thing. There is no script. There is no right or wrong way to do it. It's simply listening, holding space, withholding judgment, emotionally connecting and communicating that incredibly healing message of, 'You are not alone'.*
> *~ Brené Brown*

Like that moment I ran to Lucas's mom's home and just hugged her, saying I was sorry for ignoring her. I knew I ignored her because I didn't know what to say. I was so uncomfortable with the loss of Lucas that I created disconnect with her.

Hugging her and saying, "I'm so, so sorry," created connection for us both in our grieving moments—even to where she was able to be there so powerfully for me after the loss of Ariann.

> *Empathy is wanting people to feel connection, to have them feel that they are not alone at this time. It shows them who they can turn to, who is their grief tribe and who can be there for them in non-judgment, holding the space for them as we connect with them.*
> *~ Brené Brown*

After the death of Ari, I remember a lady saying to me, "Sweet child. Your heart has been broken apart, hasn't it?"

YES, IT HAS! I screamed inside my head.

She allowed me to be exactly where I was with no questions, no uncomfortableness—nothing but empathy.

I had a sweet neighbor show up and sit with me on the couch, while I cried my eyes out. She just sat with me in my heart-breaking moment.

One of my good friends lost her husband on a Christmas vacation in Puerto Rico. Imagine that one. No don't. Just empathize with her. At the funeral, someone said to her, "This is as sucky as it gets."

Yep nailed it.

My friend said it was the one thing she remembered during that time was that person saying, "This is as sucky as it gets."

Creating connection is really vital in all aspects of life, especially in loss. Saying the same to everyone will not always be the right words, but it sounds good to me. Empathy is so different from kindness or pity.

And don't confuse it with the Golden Rule, "Do unto others as you would have them do unto you."

As George Bernard Shaw pointed out, "Do not do unto others as you would have them do unto you—they might have different tastes." Empathy is about discovering those tastes, "[b]eing led by the spirit not knowing beforehand the things you should do" (1 Nephi 4:6-7), and stepping in to their grief and pain whole heartedly.

One of the greatest shows of empathy and creating unity was recorded by John in his impressive detail as he personally hears it fall from the lips of the Son of God at the close of the evening, after he and his apostles had dined together for the very last time:

> *Father, the hour is come; glorify thy Son, that thy Son also may glorify thee. ...*
>
> *I have manifested thy name unto the men which thou gavest me out of the world: thine they were, and thou gavest them me; and they have kept thy word. ...*
>
> *I pray for them: I pray not for the world, but for them which thou hast given me; for they are thine. ...*
>
> *Holy Father, keep through thine own name those whom thou hast given me that they may be one, as we are. ...*
>
> *As thou has sent me into the world, even so have I also sent them into the world ...*
>
> *Neither pray I for these alone, but for them also which shall believe on me through their word;*
>
> *That they all may be one; as thou, Father, art in me, and I in thee, that they also may be one in us: that the world may believe that thou hast sent me.*
>
> *And the glory which thou gavest me I have given them; that they may be one, even as we are one.* (John 17)

Right before His crucifixion, Jesus Christ washed His disciples' feet, blessed them, and prayed for them, saying, "That we may be one, even as they are."

The truest of all empathetic healers is Jesus Christ. *Being one* is a powerful way of being with someone in heartache and the mourning ride.

It's not easy, but it's so very important for a grieving journey to have someone who is 'one with you.' Someone who doesn't fully understand but can at least be with you at that time. Someone who *feels* with you. Someone who wants to connect and who honors you wherever you are in your journey.

I love the concept of being one in the grieving journey. What a difference that would've made for me as I overcame the biggest heartache of my life, Ariann Maree. That would've really been an awesome connected, mourning journey for me to have.

We are truly dependent on each other, "and the eye cannot say unto the hand, I have no need of thee: nor again the head to the feet, I have no need of you." (1 Corinthians 12:21)

As a grieving mother, I have need of you. As a grieving divorcee, I have need of you. As someone who is dealing with pain and heartache from life's challenges, I have need of you. As 2020 and 2021 ended, I have need of you.

As you are grieving and hurting, you have need of me. As you are dealing with death or difficult times, you have need of me. We are all in need of each other. We have been created to have a deep connection with each other—to not go at it alone.

"And whether one member suffer, all the members suffer with it; or one member be honored, all the members rejoice with it." (1 Corinthians 12:26)

If we are one and connected as one, we suffer when all suffer and we rejoice when all rejoice. Paul's words are as applicable to us today as they were to the saints at Corinth. Each one of us can cultivate empathy throughout our lives, through the trials and heartaches. We can then use that empathy as a radical force for social transformation.

We need a social transformation to transform the way we react, the comments we make, and the way we show up in crucial and hard times. It's time to get uncomfortable with each other and uncomfortable with those grieving. It's time to create connection in this life of struggle. We need more empathy. More people who show up with Christ-like empathy. More people ready to get out of their comfort zones and *be* with whatever it is. People who can show up and be with each other, no matter what. To connect. To see suffering and heartache, and honor it.

One of the stories of the scriptures that nails this concept head-on is when Lazarus dies, told by John in chapter 11.

Martha runs out to meet Jesus Christ and His followers crying, "Lord, if you had been here, my brother would not have died. But I know that even now, God will give you whatever you ask."

When he meets Mary, she says the same of him, "Lord, if you had been here, my brother would not have died."

The scriptures say, "When Jesus saw her weeping, and the others who had come along with her weeping also, he was deeply moved in spirit and troubled. He asked, 'Where have you layed him?' 'Come and see Lord,' they replied."

And then the shortest scripture of all, and yet one of the deepest moments of empathy and mourning happened.

In verse 35 it says, "Jesus wept."

Jesus wept. He knew He was going to raise Lazarus from the dead but he actually stopped and grieved. He had empathy with the women whom He loved, who loved their brother Lazarus, whom He loved also. He showed the greatest of empathy in that moment and just wept with them. Didn't try and change them, comfort them or do anything else—just wept with them.

Can we do this? Can we weep with those who are mourning? Can we be *one* for people who are grieving? If you're in it, you get it. If you've been through it, you got it. If you haven't, you can grow into it. Even if it is not your strength, it can be learned. I promise you. We need to change the way it is for people in grief, the things said, the 'trying to fix/change' it. We need to create connection. We need empathy.

"God gives us weaknesses so we come unto Him and become Humbled and to make our weaknesses become strong unto Him." (Ether 12:27)

In this life, in our heartaches and death, even in the day-to-day, there is a constant need for unity.

In many scriptures, Jesus Christ has asked us to be one, even as He is one with His Father.

In the scriptures it says, "For if we are not one, we are not His?" (Romans 8:9)

It's the first commandment, "Love one another, even as I have loved you." We are following His example when we are one creating unity with others. We must learn to be *one* as He has asked us to be. To be one in mourning, to be one in empathy, to be one in Him.

A few years ago, after the Paris bombing, a band came out with a song that hits it spot on for this topic.

At this time, scan this:

We Are One—*A Song For Paris & The World* - RUNAGROUND

Wow. To step in to *living* that song in our hearts and world.

One. We are one.

I stand in being able to be one with those who are grieving and for all who are going through their life's hard.

Can you?

Scan QRC to learn more about Brené Brown's work.

Journaling Thoughts

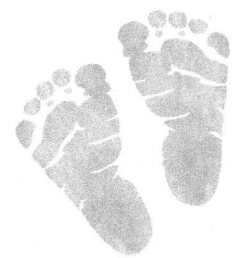

* 12 *

WHAT should I SAY?

"If you can't say somethin' nice, don't say nuthin' at all." Thumper [Disney's Bambi]

M Y SISTER, REBECCA'S FAVORITE MOVIE as a little girl was the Disney movie, *Bambi*. There's a part in that movie that became Becca's theme for her amazing and very kind life. She repeated it often to many of us.

In the epic scene, Bambi is just being born and he can't walk very well. Thumper in his cute voice, says, "He doesn't walk very good, does he?"

"Thumper," his mom says.

"Yes, Momma?"

"What did your father tell you this morning?"

Thumper's famous line that impressed Becca as a very little girl and became her life mission was, "If you can't say somethin' nice, don't say nuthin at all."

If you can't say anything nice. Don't say anything at all. That's a mission to live by.

Becca defined kindness as, "Somebody who brings warmth and value to someone with nothing expected in return."

She also said, "It doesn't matter what you say, it matters how you leave people feeling."

People will always remember what you say if what you say leaves them hurting or wounded. Most importantly people will remember how you left them feeling. How you left them feeling loved, supported, connected, and uplifted. People remember the feeling you left them with. Always.

Back to the grieving journey. The question to ask yourself as you begin to speak to someone grieving or dealing with a hard time in their life, "Is it nice?," as Thumper learned.

Really? Is it nice?

Before you answer, can I share some guidelines to assist you with this?

Is what I am going to say, kind, necessary, or helpful? Will it create connection or disconnection? Am I curious or do I really care? Do I want to leave the person feeling loved and honored or leave them confused? Will they step in to me or will they step away from me with what I am about to say? Is it kind? Is it necessary? Is it really true? Is it something they need to hear right now?

Hopefully these questions assist you in thinking about what you say to someone in grief or hard time.

As I look back at some of the statements made to me, I remember feeling touched by the beautiful words that filled me and didn't take away from me.

I remember coming back to my job after the funeral and a few weeks off to a sweet and beautiful note and money from my boss and community. She had so much love and compassion sharing with me about how so many asked about me, were praying for me, and even had left money for me. I will never forget that tender moment and the love she and my clients had for me. I still have that letter in my Ariann box.

Thinking back, I looked to the times of connection, for things said, feelings felt, and my heart touched during that time. Then thinking about what was said, what words were spoken and did they really matter, or not?

Carl Sandburg is credited with saying, "Be careful with your words, once they are said, they can only be forgiven and not forgotten."

What we say can never be taken back. Let's say words that touch and inspire.

Here is a list and some examples of appropriate comments:

- "I am so sorry for your loss."
- "I can't even imagine what you're going through or feeling."
- "This is a hard one to handle. I am so sorry."
- "My heart is breaking for you and your loss."
- "Please know you and your family are in my thoughts and prayers."
- "I have such fond memories of so-and-so."
- "Your loved one will be missed."
- "She is a precious soul and touched me."
- "When you're ready to talk, please feel free to call me." (Please actually *mean* this and check back with that one.)
- "I don't even know what to say. I am so sorry."
- "My favorite memory of your loved one is…"
- "I am here for you if you need to talk." (Also mean it and remind them of that later on.)

- "I am usually up late if you want me to come over/call me."
- "You are in my prayers."
- "I love you. I am here for you."
- "I would love to hear more about your child, your mom, your grandpa." (Sharing about them keeps them alive for us.)
- "Here is some money to assist with your expenses. Bless you all."
- Say *nuthin'*—just hug the person.

Remember, it's their choice who they bring into their space to help them. Even at certain times in your life, have you wondered who could help you the very best with what you are or were dealing with? You could be *that* for someone. You could be their angel in some of the healing if you really wanted.

I noticed how people responded to me, what I was going through, and how I stepped in to them because of the safe space they were for me at the time. It's timing and who you're being at the moment, if I'll step in and let you help me with my grief—being able to connect with you.

Whatever we do, we must choose empathy. Create connection. Let the spirit of kindness guide us to say heartfelt words not hurtful ones. Step in to the grieving soul and have them step in to us. What a gift we could be for someone by staying in kindness, acceptance, lovingly willing to mourn with and bear the burdens of another.

The Book of Mormon's Book of Mosiah, Chapter 18 is one of my favorites. Alma the Prophet, is a powerful witness of God and has a beautiful testimony of Jesus Christ.

In these scriptures, he testifies of the Savior, the resurrection of the dead, redemption of people, all because of the sufferings, and the life and death of Jesus Christ.

Alma preached to them of repentance, redemption and faith in the Lord, Jesus Christ.

In Verse 8, he has them gathered at the Waters of Mormon, giving them their covenants behind their baptisms, and he says,
> *Now, as ye are desirous to come into the fold of God, and to be called His people and are willing to bear one another's burdens, that they may be light.*

Verse 9 says,
> *Yea and are willing to mourn with those that mourn, yea and comfort those that stand in need of comfort, and to stand as a witness of God at all times and in all things, and in all place that ye may be in, even until death, that ye may be redeemed of God, and be numbered with those of the first resurrection, that ye may have eternal life.*

To mourn with those who mourn and to comfort those in need of comfort, is empathy. To bear one another's burdens, is empathy. It is part of the baptismal covenants we as members of the church make.

There is a time to mourn, even with others who mourn.

In Verse 21 of the same chapter, it says,
> *...and he commanded them that there should be no contention one with another, but that they should look forward with one eye, having one faith and one baptism, having their hearts knit together in unity and in love one towards another.*

"Having their hearts knit together in unity and in love towards one another." That is the ultimate definition of empathy. To be one with another, to feel them, to see their heartache, to mourn with them, and to be knitted together in all that they're bearing or dealing with. The ultimate way to empathy.

As you now know, one of Becca's favorite singers was Josh Groban. His soulful voice often played when we painted, tied a Christmas quilt, or just hung out.

I leave you now with his inspiring words of his song in hopes that you too can "raise the grieving up."

You Raise Me Up *by Josh Groban*

Journaling Thoughts

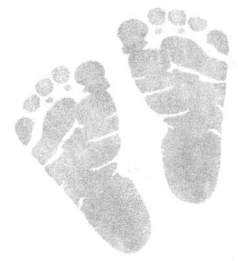

* 13 *

SUPPORTING this GRIEF

*"No one ever told me that grief felt so like fear.
I am not afraid, but the sensation is like being
afraid."* ~ *C. S. Lewis,* A Grief Observed

I DON'T OFTEN USE THE WORD, hate. Words are powerful for me. For me, hate is an intense word. Not a lot of good comes from using that word.

I don't use it, yet, saying that, I *hate* roller coasters. They freak me out. I am intensely afraid of them and of being on them. It is mostly because I like to be in control. I like to know and see what's coming. I like to make events happen on the ground—not flying uncontrollably in a car up in the air. Not my thing at all.

Quite a few years ago, my nieces and nephews begged me to go on this certain roller coaster with them. I relented. Standing in line, I was freaking out—sweating and anxiously waiting to get on the ride for a good hour. I was having a panic attack even before getting on. I almost backed out.

It finally came our time to get on. I screamed and cried the whole time. I was high and low and upside down and in and out and all over the place. I hated it! I truly despised it. I haven't gotten on another one since.

Grief is so much like that. It feels like a crazy roller-coaster ride with emotional and physical highs, lows, ups, downs, and all over the place. It's a nutty place to be emotionally, even feeling like you belong in a mental facility being monitored because of your craziness.

The out-of-control feeling is what I hate the most. *That* is grief. You're holding on to a ride at *Six Flags* or behind a ski boat on a tube wondering, *How this is going to go and when is it going to stop?*

But imagine all that confusion in a really dark place with not a lot of light—and *you* are supposed to hold on as you continue in the dark alone. Grief feels so much like the C. S. Lewis's fear quote at the beginning of this chapter.

When I read it, it hit spot on. A few days after my baby died I began to have panic attacks—fear-based panic attacks that continued for a very long time. The best way to describe the fear I felt is the feeling of being lost. Oh, so very lost. In a very dark, creepy forest with nothing around, lots of unfamiliar sounds, and not knowing how to escape or who is protecting you or what you need to be protected from. It's always dark in that forest, with no daylight. It's freaky and unnerving.

In the midst of trying to control my fears and hang on for my life, I totally forgot who I was. I lost me. And gained a permanent sense of being afraid and not knowing me.

As C. S. Lewis said so well, "The dreading of the moments when the house was so empty was when I was scared the most."

It was when I was left alone also, I found myself the most scared—even years later. We think we want to be alone, but the actual being alone is very turbulent for us in the grief journey.

For me when I was alone, panic attacks and fear went on for years and years, making it difficult to breathe. Even when the grief went away, the fear stayed for a very long time.

When my third marriage was over, I again started having panic attacks. It was fear. Feeling lost in the dark and dealing with the fear of it again.

The questions I asked at those times were, "What will I do?," "How will I make it?"

The reminder after that divorce came, "Lean on God. Lean on others. Just do the next simple step, line upon line. Here a little, there a little."

That was the message I remembered from the pain journey of burying and physically losing Ariann in this life.

That's how we do it. By small and simple actions, we walk through grief. A tiny itty-bitty step to the next step. By simply walking through the grief, the fear starts to fade, to ease, just a tiny bit. One step at a time.

Eleanor Roosevelt said, "You gain strength, courage and confidence by every experience in which you really stop to look fear in the face."

I couldn't deal or even relate to the loss and the grief with the death of our baby girl. The fear thing, the hearing babies crying, the arms physically hurting, the unsettled butterfly feelings, the constantly wired and nutty brain, the reaction to lights and sounds, surrounded by people and wanting everyone to go but dreading being alone. Sometimes, I can still feel wobbly in my life and suffer a panic attack and some anxiety in a moment because of the lingering fear. But I've learned to breathe into it all.

Once again C. S. Lewis put it beautifully,

> *An odd by-product of my loss is that I'm afraid of being an embarrassment to everyone I meet. At work, at the club, in the street, I see people, as they approach me, trying to make up their minds whether they'll 'say something about it' or not. I hate it if they do, and if they don't...*
>
> *And grief still feels like fear. Perhaps more strictly, like suspense. Or like waiting; just hanging about waiting for something to happen. It gives life a permanently provisional feeling. It doesn't seem worth starting anything. I can't settle down. I yawn, I fidget, I smoke too much. Up 'til this I always had too little time. Now there is nothing but time. Almost pure time, empty successiveness...*

This is grief. And it's all over the place. It's called the crazy, grief roller-coaster ride for this reason.

Understanding what grief is and what is common for people to feel when someone dies can help us experience a measure of peace while going through the grieving process.

- You feel so distracted as though you can't focus on anything other than your loss and the grief.
- You feel like you have to conserve your energy to deal with the emotion and stress of your grief.
- You feel as though activities you once enjoyed seem meaningless or unimportant.
- You disengage from activities because they remind you of your loved one.
- You feel anxious about seeing people/social interaction.
- You feel anxious about running into grief triggers.
- You feel anxious about becoming emotional in front of others.

- You no longer feel like a capable and competent person.
- The world no longer feels like a safe and reliable place.
- It feels safe and comfortable to not push yourself.
- Engaging in activities feels like a betrayal or as though you're "moving on".
- You think you'll feel better in time, so you decide to stay at home and wait it out.

However, we're never alone in our grief. Not only is grief common to humanity, but our God knows grief. The Word of God tells us that God the Father was grieved in His heart (Genesis 6:6), that Jesus grieved (Mark 3:5), and that the Holy Spirit can be grieved. (Ephesians 4:30)

"Jesus wept."

This great God who understands grief walks with us through the valley of the shadow of death, and He comforts us. (Psalm 23:4)

You've got God, so the real question is, "Who's your tribe?" Who is your *Support Section*? It is so important to be around people who are good for your soul.

The latest and trendy saying is, "Your vibe attracts your tribe." Your tribe is those you call in, those you trust, those you go to, those who come to you, those you want in your life and around you even in your darkest moments. Your tribe is important, especially in your time of grief.

It's been said you are the sum of the top five people you hang with. Who is your tribe? Your grief support if you need one?

It's important to share your story. Shout it out. Whisper it out. Write it out. But share your story, anyway. Some won't understand. Some will turn away from you. Yet, some will step in to you and thank you for being brave as you share your story.

Then the magic happens. One by one, people will say, "Me, too." That's when your tribe will begin gathering around you. You will feel their support and love in a way you have not felt. You will not be alone after that.

Open up and share your story.

To those of you grieving, who's in your tribe? To those of you reading this to understand us who will be in our tribe—thank you! Maybe this will better help you to understand us, to connect with us, to find a way into our sad and crazy grief world.

One of the crucial times of grieving (and when I have learned to show up for someone) is a few weeks after the funeral. After my baby had died and the funeral was all over and done, I was grateful for the lonely space after my mom left, for a moment. But I remember then feeling really alone. It felt like nobody was there for me.

In that vulnerable and alone moment, I have the memory of a friend showing up on our front doorstep a few weeks after Ariann's death. I didn't want to answer the door, but she knew I was home and wouldn't leave until I opened the door, letting her in. She came and sat with me on the couch and let me cry for hours—just sitting with me, not saying anything the whole time.

She knew.

She knew there was nothing she could say so she did the 'just be with me' thing. That made a huge difference for me. She was empathy at its shiniest moment—mourning with me at my time of mourning.

One of my friends recalled that a few weeks after the funeral of her baby, everything stopped—the food, the cards, the people coming in or even being there for her. That's when her world crashed in. She realized she was alone and hurting way too bad to be all alone.

That's when we need our tribe, our friends, and our family to show up for us. Our world has flipped upside down and we don't know which way we're standing. All we know is we are physically without the one we loved. Our brains are fighting to tell us we are the same person, nothing much has changed but this great loss. Yet our hearts scream that our whole world is done. Pretty soon our brains agree, "Okay. Our world is over."

Making it through can come back to, *who* are you connected with? Who are your people? Who could be there for you?

If you're reading this book to learn how to connect with those who have felt big loss, who could you be for one who is grieving?

We become very aware of who we're willing to let in on our very sacred journey. Not everybody is to be let in. We slowly start to hand pick people who can help us through our grief time.

For many years as I built a phenomenal health business, one of my favorite quotes had been Theodore Roosevelt, *Man in the Arena*.

> *It is not the critic who counts; not the one who points out how the strong one stumbles, or where the doer of deeds could have done them better. The credit belongs to the one who is actually in the arena, whose face is marred by dust and sweat and blood; who strives valiantly; who errs, who comes short again and again, because there is no effort without error and shortcoming; but who does actually strive to do the deeds; who knows great enthusiasms, the great devotions; who spends oneself in a worthy cause; who at the best knows in the end the triumph of high achievement, and who at the worst, if he/she fails, at least fails while daring greatly, so that his/her place shall never be with those cold and timid souls who neither know victory nor defeat.*

If you've buried someone you love, *you* are in the arena. It's not a comfortable place to be, yet being in the arena is where we find our true selves, connection, hope, light—and a new way of living. It's the place of being real and vulnerable, finding the connection we need to thrive through the being-in-the-grief arena.

In her *Daring Greatly* book, Brené Brown says, "We all step into an arena every day."

That concept really resonates with me—what Brené calls the *arena* metaphor.

Being in the grief arena requires us to be uncomfortable, vulnerable, and open. It feels that way especially with the grief journey. We are being fully seen, open, raw, and feeling broken. Courage is a value we must hold to.

Brené says about this time, "If *you* are not in the arena getting *your* butt kicked, I am *not* interested your feedback."

There are no cheap seats in the arena. Feedback is *not* a way of creating connection with those of us in the arena. It can feel like an attack, like a blame, like a problem to be solved.

Brené says, "Vulnerability is not winning or losing; it's having the courage to show up and be seen when we have no control over the outcome. Vulnerability is not weakness; it's our greatest measure of courage."

Let's explore your arena. Would you do an exercise with me?

I want you to close your eyes for a minute and visualize a huge arena—one you have visited or would like to visit.

The Utah Jazz arena in Salt Lake City is a good one for me to visualize. I've been there and can easily see it. It sits 18,000 people. It's huge.

Visualize whatever arena you've been to or can see in your mind's eye. After you see your arena, shift your vision and think of that arena as some aspect of your life. If you've lost a baby or child recently, take to it that grieving in your life right now. Or some other aspect of your life. Whatever it be, it could even be a divorce or a financial loss.

Take a minute to consider a few thoughts: What does the arena look like for you? How do you want to show up in your arena? How do you want to be seen in that arena?

I believe the arena's support section—the source of empathy and self-compassion—holds the most important seats. It's where we go for sustenance and the energy to carry on. Who is seated in your support section?

Answer these questions to figure out who occupies the front row of your support section:

- To whom do I turn when I am getting beaten down in that arena?
- Who lifts me up, dusts me off, and sends me back in to fight?
- Who cheers me on and is proud to be there?
- Do I cheer for myself? Or do I give myself confusing messages about what I should've done or said instead?
- Who lets me grieve the way I am grieving?
- Do I let myself grieve wholly?
- Who does not let me be a victim around that grief and in my life?
- Do I let myself be a victim?

Once I answer those questions, I focus on the "front row" people in my support section. I see their faces—the ones I can trust or who will step forward during my raw time.

You might know some. You might not yet know some.

Who is in your support section? Place the names in the box. I make a point to sit in my own self-compassion and empathy seats. I am my biggest support in my support section. Are *you* in yours?

Place your name in the box if you are your biggest supporter.

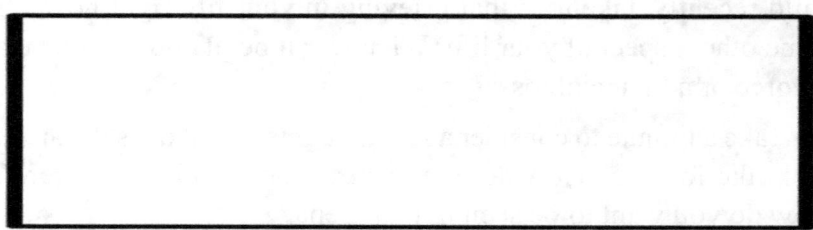

Who's in your box?

Right now in your grief, you might not be your biggest support and that's okay. I challenge you to work toward changing that, to see yourself as your biggest cheerleader sitting in your support section cheering yourself on. That just means you get up and stand up for you. Give yourself some daily self-care. Keep finding your way.

Those few actions could be all it takes to step into the arena for yourself at this time.

Can you possibly step into that arena for *you*? I hope so.

I love the song sung by Matthew West: *Hello, My Name Is*.

Stand in the knowledge you are a child of the One True King and what you say to you matters, especially during the healing time.

It is not selfish or greedy for you to love and support you and to focus on your true happiness as you find your healing grace. It is necessary.

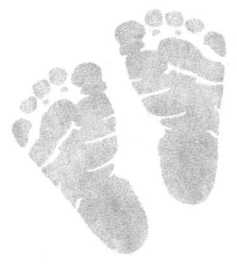

* 14 *

STAGES of GRIEF

"Grief is like the ocean; it comes in waves, ebbing and flowing. Sometimes the water is calm and sometimes the water is overwhelming. All we can do is learn to swim as it is." Vicki Harrison

IN THE BEGINNING, THEY TOLD me there were *stages* to my grief. Elisabeth Kübler-Ross introduced us to the concept, "The first six months of grief will be marked by denial, anger, bargaining, depression, and acceptance."

Remember the *acceptance* chapter? What they don't tell you about those five stages of grief is you will experience all of them in one day and sometimes every day in multiple waves, one after the other. We don't all go through each stage in the same order. Even in the first months it doesn't look the same for anyone.

There are also many additional stages of grief. Everyone grieves differently. Grief's unexpected turns creep up again and again even years later.

At least, that's how it was for me. Sometimes I would cycle through all of them repeatedly in a day. It's exhausting—emotionally twisted and turning.

You feel you've stepped forward. Then you get triggered or knocked back. The jolt can take you two steps back, or even more. You step forward again. A song plays that reminds you of your loss, and you're knocked down again. A birthday or holiday comes and kicks your butt yet again.

You are in the arena.

Another trial happens or someone else passes away and your grief wound is again ripped open—feels like salt being dumped on it. You realize you didn't completely heal the first time. Like an onion, the grief healing process is layer-by-layer. You feel all the emotions throughout the next six months to a year, or longer, taking the roller-coaster ride up and down.

You are riding the grief ride and its track goes all over the place.

The five stages of grief are a tool to give us hope along the journey. It will take some time to move through the denial, the anger, the bargaining, the depression, and into acceptance.

I believe there is a next step—a step in to finding true hope and a new purpose. [More to come on this.] It's when we begin to look ahead, feeling like we can go on, finding ourselves laughing and smiling and stepping in to the "New Norm" of our life without the one we love.

When I long for my past, I ache for Ariann and our life together. The ache brings feelings of loneliness, anxiety, and heartache. When I look in to my unknown future, I am overwhelmed with anxiety and plead for answers. Those emotions bring feelings of despair and doubt, and at times leaves me feeling forgotten and alone.

When the children of Israel were lost in the wilderness, God blessed them with manna. They were given enough to be fed one day at a time. God provided for the daily needs of his covenant people. He wanted them to focus on the *here* and *now*.

When I step in my day-by-day moments, I am partaking of the daily manna God gives to me. Every day I have a choice to receive God's daily bread. His daily nourishment. In each moment.

Don't let worrying about the future or focusing on the past rob you of your daily bread from God. Receiving daily bread is a choice we must make. I have chosen to put my faith in Christ and His promises. I have chosen to find joy, even in a life I never imagined—a life without the one I love. We all have a choice to focus on the moment—no past and no future in our space.

A quote by Walt Whitman says, "Happiness, not in another place, but this place. Not for another hour, but for this hour."

Today could be the day to feel acceptance, hope, and joy.

"Take heart: weeping may tarry for the night, but joy comes with the morning. Christ turns our mourning into dancing." (Psalms 30:5 & 11)

There *will* be *joy in the morning*. I am learning there can also be joy in the *mourning*. Joy in the mourning is the example my parents taught me years after my baby died, when their daughter died. They were strong and living in the moment of their joy in the mourning.

As A. W. Tozer said, "When I understand that everything happening to me is to make me more Christ-like, it resolves a great deal of anxiety."

Mourning and grief are some of the deepest expressions of the purest kind of love. Know it is so okay to grieve and to mourn. You loved deeply. Grief is all the love you had to give and now are not able to give. It comes out as mourning.

"Grief is all that unspent love gathered up in the corners of your eyes, the lump in your throat, and that hollow part of your chest. Grief is just love with no place to go." ~ Jamie Anderson

The Savior has said, "Thou shalt live together in love, insomuch that thou shalt weep for the loss of them that die." (D&C 42:45)

I've learned grief is the price we pay for loving someone—and the price is so very worth it. Nobody I have known would ever give up the love they had for a family member in order to avoid the grief that came with losing that family member. When loved ones pass from this side to the other, they continue to be just as important to us as when they were with us. Because we love them, we can't really expect to completely "get over" losing them.

When talking about grief—it's not something you can measure or put on a time-line No one should say or judge how it goes for you or me. Time does not heal this wound. The wound does eventually scar over but it's always there. Time just masks it a little bit, here and there. Until its slightly band-aided over. But it's a tender place that in any moment, with any song, any question or memory, friends getting married or having kids, or so many things, it could rip right open and be raw and, oh, so very painful.

That's the real part of mourning. It's deep.

It lasts a lifetime.

Even thirty years later, Faith Hills, *Where Are You Christmas* makes me ugly-cry. Boom. Mourning. Raw. Open. In the Arena.

Still.

Again.

Some people will move though grief faster. Some slower. It really depends on the death, the way it happened, and a myriad other circumstances. No two people are the same in their grief.

Grief comes in waves of emotions. When we are doing the dishes, getting ready for work, driving a car or watching a movie—all of a sudden it hits us again with full force—so very much—how much we miss the one we lost. The tears flow and the sadness is so great it's truly physically painful to go on in the moment.

The only people who think there is a time limit for grief have never lost a piece of their heart. We need to be encouraged to take all the time we need. You, who have not lost that deeply, need to allow those you love their time to be in their space. It's their journey of grief and heartache. We can't tell them what it looks like or how much time it will take. It will take as long as it takes. This is their winter.

Like the book [*To Heal Again* by Rusty Berkus] my sister gave me said,

> *You sit in the shadow of sorrow seeking, searching for the magic that will make the pain go away. Weep what you must weep, not only for this loss, but for all other losses you have sustained in this life. Surrender into the memory of what once was and can no longer be. This winter of your life will pass, as all seasons do. Stay in your season of Winterness as long as you need be, for everything that you feel is appropriate. There is no right way to grieve—there is just your way. It will take as long as it takes. It is important to be ever so gentle, kind, loving and giving to yourself right now and to let others be ever so gentle, kind, loving and giving to you.*

One of the phrases I said over and over again in the first year is, "I don't care. I don't care. I don't care."

I found this to be the statement that profoundly shut me down and gave me an excuse to not want to live my life. I still find myself saying it, even thirty years later. I have to recognize it's one of the side-effects grief instilled in me—an "I don't care" excuse to step out of my life.

Yet, I do care. It's just in the moments of life's really hard stuff that my victim story comes creeping up again. I have to tell myself to *stop* and tell my brain to *be quiet*—my heart *does* care. I do want to be alive and in this life feeling all the pains, joys, and hopes.

When talking about grief, we must also talk about the power of the body physically suffering from the emotional toll on it. In much of my studying and holistic coaching in health and wellness over the last twenty years, I have learned, "what happens on an emotional level will affect us on a physical level."

Dr Candace Pert, Neuroscientist says,
Most psychologists treat the mind as disembodied, a phenomenon with little or no connection to the physical body. Conversely physicians treat the body with no regard to the mind or the emotions. But the body and mind are not separate, and we cannot treat one without the other.

She also says,
Repressed traumas caused by overwhelming emotion can be stored in a body part, thereafter affecting our ability to feel that body part or even move it.

The body and the mind and the heart are not separate. The emotional hit of a loss will have an impact on the physical body. Be prepared. Especially in the first few months of your great loss.

Dr Pert adds,
As our feeling change, this mixture of peptides travels throughout your body and your brain. Literally changing the chemistry of every cell in your body.

I was given a book years ago when I was suffering with the grief of Ariann, titled, *Feelings Buried Alive Never Die* by Karol Kuhn Truman. It's a phenomenal read. It really hits this subject head-on.

Karol writes,
> *Everything you have ever felt, believed, said or done, heard or experienced has been recorded and registered in your body somewhere. If your feelings, thoughts or beliefs have been negative regardless of the intensity—it makes no difference. They have all registered in every fiber, nook and cranny of your BE-ing! Yes, it has all been recorded of the DNA of the cells of your glands, your blood, your lymph system, your organs and your muscles... your flesh...*

In Karol's book, she lists the physical ailments and emotions associated with those physical ailments. For *Anxiety*, the emotions are: "Feels unable to 'call the shots' in life, Feels boxed in, Feels helpless to affect a change."

Does that not sound like the emotions of losing a baby? Especially for a control freak, like me. Yep—pretty spot on!

Karol says *Anger* weakens the liver. *Grief* weakens the lungs. (Does it feel like you can't breathe in your grief?) *Worry* weakens the stomach. *Stress* weakens the heart and brain. *Fear* weakens the kidneys. Not many physicians will talk about the emotional aspect of grief that affects us physically. None of mine did.

There are many signs of trapped emotions including joint pain, skin issues, chronic fatigue, addictive behaviors, Irritable Bowel Syndrome (IBS), anger or short tempered, feelings of anxiety or ongoing depression, shoulder/neck/back tension or pain, compulsive and impulsive behaviors, digestive issues, auto-immune diseases—these can all be feelings buried alive.

Sigmund Freud stated, "Unexpressed emotions will never die. They are buried alive and will come forth later in uglier ways."

One of the side-effects of the mourning journey is emotional effect on our body. What happens on an emotional level will affect us on a physical level. I have seen this again and again. In myself as well as in my clients, friends, and family. We must remember this *key* piece as we are healing: *Do not bury the emotions.* Don't avoid the triggers. Cry. Feel the pain. Feel the heartbreak. Scream. Write it out. Burn it. Go to therapy. Scream and cry some more. Do what you have to do to release *all* of the emotions from your body so they do not get buried and come back to physically bite you later.

Sadly, avoiding triggers will not create the *whole* healing that needs to happen. Whole healing only happens when we are triggered and we're able to move through the pain, the patterns, the story, and step onto a different pathway on our journey.

Christiane Northrup said,
> *Your beliefs and thoughts are wired into your biology. They become your cells, tissues, and organs. There is no supplement, no diet, no medicine, and no exercise regimen that can compare to the power of your thoughts and beliefs. That's the very first place to look when anything goes wrong in your body.*

Hmmmm... Wow! Interesting, as I look back at the intense anxiety attacks after Ariann passed and the headaches and illnesses I constantly had.

> *When we skip over our pain, and go straight to positivity, it is like floating on the surface of the ocean. Looking for a treasure that only exists in the depths; you cannot reach dawn without walking through the night. A seed is planted in darkness before it grows toward the light.* ~ *Allie Michelle,* Explorations of a Cosmic Soul.

It's said we must go through storms to experience rainbows. Listen up! You really *want* to release from your body and let go of the emotions you're carrying around. They will literally kill you if you don't.

I know that statement might be a relief for those of us in the beginning of our grief ride. But trust me, we all have something to do with our life still—a mission to fulfill beyond this moment. We need you to finish it.

Broken bread is given to broken people to make them whole. Broken people make a difference for other broken people. God uses those who are broken to rescue the *broken*. Look at me. Broken, yet I still can and I do color bright and bold.

One of the songs that I love is *Everybody Hurts*, by R.E.M. Scan this and *feel* the emotions as you cry and let some of them go.

You are not alone.

Everyone hurts and everyone cries—or at least we all should, at times. Let the cry be. Let it happen.

Whenever it does, just be with it.

Journaling Thoughts

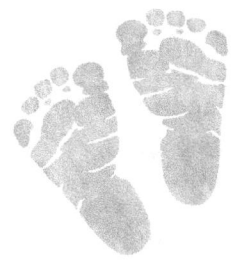

* 15 *

FIRSTS are SO NOT EASY

"Never give up—however deep the wounds of your soul, whatever their source, wherever or whenever they happen, and however short or long they persist, you are not meant to perish spiritually. You are meant to survive spiritually and blossom in your faith and trust in God." ~ Neil L Anderson

I FEEL LIKE, THE BIGGEST YEAR of grief is dealing with the *firsts* without the one we love. First Mother's Day without her. First birthday without her. First Christmas without her. First Thanksgiving without her. First anniversary without her. The *firsts* seriously suck!

They remind us again of our loss in a very long year of days of firsts without the one we love. Expect to step on to the roller-coaster ride with your year of *firsts*. When people tell me it's their first year, I pray for them all year long. It is a difficult year, for sure.

To those who support us—please be there for us in the firsts. It's not over. Even though the firsts are difficult for us, we still want to remember and to be asked about them—they are still in our hearts and in our souls, forever. They still mean so much to us.

Be comfortable with our grieving *firsts*. They still have birthdays, still remember us on holidays, still makes us mothers, still have anniversaries. We need you there for us and with us in those times.

Asking again, "Are you okay?" on any of our firsts is not a connection question. Acknowledge the firsts for the grieving souls you are supporting. Ask them if they are doing something special for their firsts. Ask them how they want you to show up and support them in their firsts. Keep asking all year long.

My first Mother's Day was my first time celebrating it as a mother and yet, no baby to show for it. That was a very difficult Mother's Day. I remember my resentment and anger for other mothers who had their babies in their arms.

My first anniversary of Ariann's death and Christmas Day was coming up. I was a single and pregnant women, having no contact with my babies' father. I was hurting with the reminder of the first year coming to a close and the anniversary date coming, being alone.

As I was expressing to my therapist my heartfelt concerns for the firsts and how to acknowledge the first year, he said something so beautiful and so perfect for me.

He said, "Why not honor her with a gift for you of what her memory means to you."

So I did.

That first Christmas, I spent a lot of time finding the perfect and sweetest gift I could for her and me. The first gift I bought was a *Precious Moments* figurine of an angel sitting on a cloud throwing hearts down from heaven saying, SENDING YOU ALL MY LOVE.

I still have it. It's precious to me. It meant so much to me to find that precious gift. I also bought her a sweet Christmas bear, that had the year, 1991 on it—my first Christmas without her.

Every year after, I have bought her another *Precious Moments* angel or part of a nativity and a Christmas bear. It has been a treasured gift for me to have and to remind me she's with me. Always.

My mom also has so much fun trying to find the perfect Christmas bear for me every year. I have thirty-plus Christmas bears now that are a sweet reminder of Ari's precious life and the gift she is in my life.

My actual *first* Christmas was spent in complete heartache and tears. I was pregnant and not married, which would have made it even harder. But the reminder of the day and the heartache of not having Ariann with me was so fricken difficult. Firsts are so, so hard.

The anniversary date of a loved one's death is particularly significant. We have done something we thought was totally impossible many months earlier. We have survived an entire year without someone as important to us as life itself. Those of you who support us, thank you for doing so. We hit a significant mile marker for us. Keep remembering we are still hurting and making our way through our mourning journey, and it is so not over.

Into the second year, life starts to feel a bit 'norm' again or at least the 'new normal' you've created. Moments of joy will return and go away. We will cry, get angry, and despair again when we see reminders, hear the songs, see the pictures, the clothes and cherished possessions of the one who died. We still might not have cleaned out their room and all their stuff and it's okay. It's not time until it's time. Let it be.

We do not need to be reminded about their stuff in the closets or rooms. We know. We're working our way toward it. Mom kept my little sister's belongings in her closet for years and years. It was no one's place, including me, to tell Mom how long was right or wrong in letting her things go.

In the third year, hopefully we slowly begin to construct a 'new normal' life and move to finding peace and standing in hope. The memories continue to return and we cry and break down when we hear certain songs, watch a movie, or see other small or large reminders. Holidays and birthdays will still take us out of the game of life and right back in that dang grief ride.

That being said, there is no rhyme or reason to any of it. Do not hold anyone to it. Do not tell them where they should or should not be. Grief has its own individual timeline. There is *no* other way but in our own time.

One of the hardest words to hear are, "You should be getting over this," or "You should not still be feeling this way."

Exactly how we feel or where we are is exactly how we feel or where we are. No telling us to move on, get over it, find something or someone new or *blah, blah, blah.*

You, our support section must have complete *acceptance* for us and how we are or how we are not. There may be a time of intervention if destructive behavior is happening, but that's not my place to say how or my specialty. Consult a professional if you are feeling you need more information or if those you are supporting need one.

Other hard statements we keep having to hear are, "Time to move on," and "Time heals all wounds."

Sorry to say this again, but time *does not* heal the wounds. Time eases it. It lessens the pain and heartache. But, it does not *ever* heal it. Thirty years later and I still feel the deep tender wound. Sometimes it is as real as the very beginning. Time to move on is when I say, or feel, or when *I* am ready. To move on with my life has to be *my* choice.

There's a song that when it comes on the radio, I am a blubbering heartbroken momma—right back in that moment, that Christmas morning when I found her. Sometimes that's how grief goes. As fresh as the day it went down. Time is definitely a gift we all get but, once again, it does not heal the wound. We will never quite be the same and that is so totally okay. Accept us, please.

> *The reality is that you will grieve forever. You will not 'get over' the loss of a loved one; you will learn to live with it. You will heal and you will rebuild yourself around the loss you have suffered. You will be whole again but you will never be the same. Nor should you be the same nor would you want to. ~ Elisabeth Kubler Ross*

When we, as a tribe step in to knowing this, knowing we will all get through the first and the second year—and beyond if we just keep connecting, supporting, and loving—this is game changing for the grieving.

Time to scan a song to inspire and move you.

Mariah Carey, Boyz II Men singing One Sweet Day.

This song struck me hard one day as I drove down the road. It came on the radio and I cried for Rebecca June Cottam.

I miss you, Becca.

JOURNALING THOUGHTS

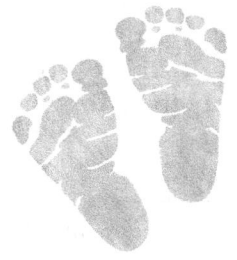

* 16 *

THERE is a TIME for THERAPY

"Therapy isn't a scary place for crazy people to go, it's a safe space for people who want to be their best self." ~ Unknown

THERE IS A STORY ABOUT the 'optimist' in the book, *Man's Search for Meaning* and the story of Viktor Frankl in the concentration camps in World War Two.

There were certain ones in the concentration camps that kept saying, "We'll be out by Christmas," or "this next holiday." And then those anticipated times would come and go and they were not out. And it actually killed them because they were *too* hopeful, *too* optimistic—expecting it to happen. This concept is quite interesting to me. Let's talk more about this within the grieving process.

Although positivity is in my top strengths, I still feel like sometimes I'm quite pessimistic. For me when my baby died, there wasn't a lot of hope. There just wasn't. There wasn't anything I held on to for hope during that time. I was not centered in Jesus Christ and God at the time. It just was day by day, in and out, up and down, high and low—depending on the day for me. Not much to hold on to hope for me.

Thinking back and feeling back to that time, there wasn't a lot of optimism in my life. I kept asking the questions, "How do I survive this?," "Can I survive this?," "Do I really want to survive this?," "Do I even want to live beyond this? Without her?"

But I did survive it. What was it that helped me persevere through it? Surviving through it? And now thriving in the loss of her and so much more in my life?

Some days during that time, I didn't even get out of bed. Some days, I didn't even get dressed. Some days, all I could think about was the pain. The heartache, the hurt. The *huge* loss. The physical pain. The intense loneliness. The ache in my arms and in my heart. Oh, the hurt. *It hurt so bad.* All I wanted to do was cry, scream, hit someone, sleep, die, repeat.

Returning back to work was oh, so difficult. Everyone knew me. Talking about my loss behind my back—or so I felt like they were. I felt like I had the plague or something. No one related to me. Yet everyone felt like they related to me or thought they knew what I was going through.

Is this what crazy feels like? Confused? Lonely? Angry? Hurt? Freaking out? I can't go on.

How do I get out of this life? How do I go on? Why would I want to go on?

Then there was the father of Ariann. I judged him and the way he was grieving. I was not sitting in his support section. Sadly, he wasn't for me, either. Why did it seem he was okay? Why didn't he cry and scream and hit someone? [Not that I ever hit anyone, even though I really wanted to.] Why wasn't he feeling all the crazy like I was? Or was he? I never really knew. He didn't say much of anything about it.

A man's grief is so different than a woman's—it is not comparable. I seriously did not understand the way he grieved. He didn't want to talk about her. I did. Pictures came down. I wanted them up. I wanted to go to therapy. He made fun of that. He did not want to talk to anyone. Bless his heart. [I say that the way my Nana says it, with complete love for him and his grieving way.]

We all grieve so totally different. I didn't understand that at the time. We did not connect in our grief rides. We did not connect at all, which made it even more difficult for us to get through it. In the first year of grieving the loss of our baby, we didn't/couldn't make the marriage work.

That was a whole other level of grief. Not only to lose my baby, I found myself going through a divorce with the man I thought I was going to be with forever. Then in the midst of all of that, I found out I was pregnant—a complete shock. He was not okay with having another one right then. I certainly wasn't either, but what choice did we have?

It was not an easy time—we celebrated our second anniversary, ordered pizza, packed up our stuff, and headed out of the marriage. Two years into our marriage, at twenty-two and twenty-four we had had a baby, buried that baby, were pregnant with another one, and were getting out of the marriage altogether.

After that moment, I realized I needed some therapy. I did not feel like I was moving forward. I was completely afraid of the future, afraid of being a single mom, afraid of having another baby, afraid of losing that baby, too.

Afraid, afraid, afraid. I was so afraid. I was living in all that fear. *Intense Fear.* C. S. Lewis would've been proud of that fear. Or would he have?

So, I put myself in therapy. I knew at that young of age we repeat what we don't repair. I did not know how to repair it but I knew emotionally I was not okay and I needed help.

I remember that first day telling the seemingly young therapist, Matt my story.

Starting with the obvious, as he could see I was pregnant. Then, continuing with telling him the story of my baby dying on Christmas Day, her being only four months old—our first born, and now going through a divorce. I told him I knew I was stuck in the past and not able to even move forward, being pregnant—wondering *how* to move forward into my future. Stuck in the past, I so felt.

I remember seeing this poor guy's jaw drop and all he could say was, "WOW!"

I also remember screaming inside, "How the heck is this guy going to help me? Seriously, what can he do to make this any better?"

We starting talking about the intense heartache, what that was like with the grief and the loss of losing Ariann on Christmas morning. I was really wanting to work through the pain and hopelessness of the future I felt.

I spent many weeks talking about Ariann, the divorce, why I was there, and trying to work through all the emotions that had so intensely impacted me. I was still struggling with the overwhelming loss and harsh mourning for many months into that first year.

There was one day, as I was talking about the future, he said, "What are you afraid of?"

He had hit it on the head. *Fear*. I was living in *fear*.

I said, "Well, I've got this baby coming and I should be looking into the future. Yet, I feel like I'm living in the past. I feel like I can't let go of Ariann and I don't want to let go of Ariann. I don't want to move on. I'm afraid of moving on. I'm afraid of forgetting her. I'm afraid of so much. I'm afraid of not having that memory. I am so afraid of the unknown. The 'what is going to happen now'? The unknown ahead of me. The *what ifs* are so haunting me."

I had finally admitted all those fears, sitting there in his office that day. By finally acknowledge what was so, life could maybe shift to acceptance and move forward.

I remember a profound exercise he had me do. He had me stand up and turn to the wall behind me.

He said, "So, I want you to just look at this, this back wall here and I want you to see your past. I want you to see Ariann and the beautiful gift she was and the life she had. And the life you had with her and her dad. I want you to see your baby's father. I want you to see this past and honor it. Be grateful for it.

"Now I want you to glance over your shoulder and I want you to see the future. I want you to see the future of *this* baby. I want you to see the hope, the light in it—to see this baby, healthy and growing. I want you to see you finding someone, stepping into a new life. I want you to see that."

"Now," he said, "I want you to look back at the wall, look at Ariann, look at that past, look at all that was and had been. Then glance over your shoulder and see this future, the new baby, the potential, the opportunities of life, the future, and all it holds for you. Look back at that past and now look forward to what is possible ahead."

"See all of that," he said. And then he said, 'I want you to turn around, step in, and face that future."

So, there I was, facing the wall of my past. The hurts, the pains and the life that was no longer. The death of a baby and a marriage and the hopes of all of that gone.

Then glancing over my shoulder and seeing the future, the hope, the new baby in a new possibility of life. I was *facing* the wall of the past and yet glancing back over my shoulder at the future ahead.

This went on for quite a while. Yet, I could not turn and face the future as he had asked me to. I could not pivot and move into that future. I was so stuck in my past.

I stood there for the longest time not able to turn, not able to step into what was possible. I know that sounds silly but I was frozen in the past.

I just stood there looking at Ari, feeling like I would betray her, forget her—feeling like I wasn't ready to say goodbye to her. Feeling the guilt of the marriage gone and the *mom guilt* of losing her. I could not turn and physically look at the future. I just couldn't do it. I stood there for quite a long while.

He asked, "What is holding you back?"

And then asked again.

I didn't know.

My therapist said, "Just turn in to it. Pivot and turn and look at your future."

I thought, *I can't step into this. How do I do this? How do I leave Ari like this?*

I was so afraid. Afraid to have another baby—*What if?* Afraid to love fully again. Afraid to give my whole heart again. I was so *afraid* to step in to what was possible for fear of losing *it all* again.

I glanced over my shoulder to look at it—to look at that future. To try and see the hope. To see the love. To see the possibility. Seeing it again and again and again and visually seeing some potential in *that* future, in *faith* in that moment.

He said, "Come on, turn in to the moment so you can face your beautiful future."

I finally did it. I physically turned around and I stepped into my future. And, it felt good. Real good. With wholehearted *faith*. It felt right and hopeful.

It was then that I felt a bit okay. It felt really good to physically turn and see ahead, see the hope of a new baby, a new life, a new love, a new heart, a 'new norm' of a life without Ariann.

It seems really silly now as I look back at my journal entry of it and that day, but it seriously had an impact on me, turning to my future, facing it with *faith* not *fear*—trusting it was all going to be okay.

One of my favorite scriptures I have hanging in my bedroom says, "For I know the plans I have for you, declares the Lord, plans to prosper you and not to harm you, plans to give you hope and a future." (Jeremiah 29:11)

I felt a beautiful message rush into my body in that moment and I stepped powerfully into it. It was amazing.

The next week, I showed up and I was happy. I really was. I was alive and I was excited. Excited for the future. Excited for what was ahead. Excited for the hope of that baby. Actually excited to be alive again.

The next week I had more excitement and more hope. Stepping into the future was so impactful for me.

The next time I came in, Matt looked at me and said, "I think you're good. Are you good? We're done for now, right?"

I remember feeling I was good. I had stepped into the possibility of my future. And it wasn't to say that I was over her. It wasn't to say I had moved on. It was just me stepping forward to what was possible. It was not easy.

As searching as that was for me, it was so impactful to step into that future, taking a baby step forward. Very necessary. Moving to what was possible, into that future moment. Not easy. Not easy at all. Yet, doable for anybody. Because I did it, anyone can do it.

My precious second-born baby girl, Emalee Kaye Jacobs was born at 6:18PM on February 1st and she became my everything.

She graced this world with a presence that took my breath away. I so wish I could say I was completely healed when I had her, but despite my brokenness, *I loved her beyond words*. She was so tiny and so very beautiful. She still is.

I am forever grateful she came to me. She saved me. She opened me up to wholly and completely love again. She was my teacher and I was her student. She continues to teach me. I continue to learn from her. She still lights me up.

Her angelic way into this world healed me beyond words. She became my whole life and all that was important to me. She is still the biggest contributor to my life. My cheerleader. My best friend. *My life.* Thank you, God for her in your time. May she know how truly grateful I am for her and her amazing *gift* of giving *life* back to me.

I was still afraid of losing her but I adored her. I still do.

After the incident above with the therapist, I realized I had really moved on well and didn't need him every week, but I still needed to talk about it to people who understood what I was going through. As I finished therapy, I joined the SIDS support group. That made such a difference for me in all we connected on and spoke about in those weekly meetings.

The people in my SIDS support group became my people, my tribe for a while. They understood me. They knew somewhat of what I was feeling. It felt so good to be heard and understood by others. To not feel so alienated and lonely, but to feel like I belonged after Ariann's death with others who understood a similar path.

I met a darling friend in the group who had buried her little boy two days after me. He died December 27th, 1990. I really loved her and our connection.

Maybe finding a support group will help you to think straight or assist in finding a 'new norm' of life. Life after the death. Support groups offer valuable support and resources to help manage your grief. Support groups can do this for those of you grieving.

I hope you find your tribe, your *ones* who can hear you and begin to facilitate some healing in you as you step forward into your 'new norm' of life.

Connection is so necessary and such a gift in the grief journey. As 2020 came to an end, *Praise the Lord*, I thought back to how much that year showed us how much we miss connection and being with people. We need it as people. We thrive from it. It is necessary for life and it is definitely necessary in grieving.

The song that touches my heart and reminds me of Ariann every time is Faith Hills, *Where are you Christmas?*

This song reminds me she is there inside my heart, filling me with love, with hope, with light as she daily guides me through life. Emalee and I love this song. We sing it at the top of our lungs whenever it comes on. I dedicate this one to Emalee and Ariann, my two angel girls, one in heaven and one still living her amazing life.

Ariann Maree, my butterfly. I'll hold you in my heart, until I hold you again in time.

Emalee Kaye, my rose. I love you with all my heart and soul.

Journaling Thoughts

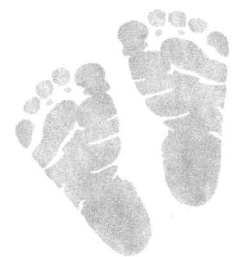

* 17 *

WHAT are YOU CARRYING in YOUR BACKPACK?

"We can't change the trail we have in life, but we can make the hike easier if we change what's in our pack." ~ John Bytheway

WE ALL HAVE 'STORIES' WE carry around with us. Events that happened or words that were said which created an impact on us—sometimes in a not-so-positive way. Some are even negative stories. Do you know what I am talking about? The story is usually the victim or sad part of our life and is what can hold us back from connecting and being our true selves.

One of my 'stories' happened when I was five years old. I did something wrong or bad and had a moment that I was reprimanded by an adult in my life and I said to my five-year-old self, "I'm a bad bad girl." (Double bad)

It was nobody's fault at all—it happens in all young lives. Yet, because of this, I believed I was a bad girl for a very long time. I then spent many years proving that 'bad girl' story to be true. Hanging with bad boys and doing 'bad girl' things. I spent my younger life not being a good girl as I was raised to be because I thought from that five-year-old's messed-up story that I was bad. I was a bit on the rebellious side as a teenager and young adult, definitely proving my bad girl story right. Kind of nutty what one little five-year-old's story can do to a life.

Because of all of that and my story, I was always quite confused about my Christian religious upbringing. It didn't make sense to me because of who I thought, as a broken little girl, I was. By the time I married my babies' father, I was finally stepping back into my spiritual self. Or, so I thought.

I was looking to my Christian upbringing for peace and tradition for our little upcoming family. We together, started to do the *right thing* in our eyes and to follow our parent's example—to follow their Christian ways, as we raised our little family. We went to church every Sunday and even taught the youth Sunday school class as we were called to do. Which is where I met sweet Lucas, whom I shared about in earlier chapters.

When we found out we were having our first child, we were so happy. We were excited to start our family. As I said, I loved being pregnant. I was very mindful of what I was eating and drinking. No soda. Less Sugar. No Medicine. I was very conscious of what went into my body, trying to give her the very best start I possibly could.

I loved having her inside of me. Growing her was a gift. I loved every minute of being pregnant with her. I worked on all of the 'important for my health and my body' work but missed the mindset development.

When Ariann was born and placed in my arms, I immediately loved her. Immensely. As she nestled there in my arms, she was angelic and perfect. Too perfect. She was straight from God and so precious and beautiful to me. She was such a perfect angel baby in every way.

Since I still had not dealt with that story of, "I'm a bad girl," I carried it around with me.

As she laid there in my arms, the negative voice in my head said, "She's too perfect, you don't deserve her."

Ahhhhh, crap. That negative voice in my head was one I listened to way too much.

That Christmas morning, as I looked at her on the floor as my husband was trying to resuscitate her, that negative voice in my head said, "Yep, that's what you deserve."

Can you believe that *that* was what I believed?

I spent many years believing I did not deserve her and she was *too* 'perfect' for me. See why that comment can trigger me?

Years later, I heard a funny story told by a scoutmaster who was taking a bunch of young kids on a long hike. They had their backpacks on as they headed up the hill. As they hiked the hardest part of the hike, one young boy kept complaining about the weight of his backpack and how he just couldn't go on. So, the scoutmaster took the boy's backpack and put it on his own back. He then realized the boy's backpack was 'way too heavy' for the few basic items in it.

"Son, what's in your backpack?"

"Well, sir," the boy said, "I have been picking up some cool rocks on the way up to take home."

The scoutmaster opened up the backpack. Sure enough, it was filled with rocks—lots of big treasure rocks the boy had been carrying up the trail to take back down with him. [My brother Tom literally does this as we hike with him.]

Sadly, it's what we do on a daily basis with our *stuff*. We weigh ourselves down with the baggage we've picked up over the years, telling ourselves we have to keep it. That it's *truth*. We need to hold on to *this* or *that* because it's who we are. We carry the stories, the mean words said to us, or the hurts we felt and saw for *way* too long.

It's what I did in telling myself I didn't deserve her. I weighed down my own backpack through my own choices.

How much does your backpack weigh? Do you feel the weight of that bag? It's heavy, and you don't need to carry all that weight around. What have you picked up in your life or around the death of your loved one that you are carrying around with you? Is it time to empty your backpack and find peace?

Kind of like me saying, "I didn't deserve that precious baby," and "I did deserve her dying."

Hard stuff to carry around. That's the baggage (the rocks) I needed to dump.

It's probably time for all of us to dump some items out of our backpacks. Or, have you upgraded to a large suitcase to drag it all?

So, what's your story surrounding the death of the one you loved? Do not let the negative thought patterns stay. Challenge them.

Talking about the loss of our loved ones and the memories of them is healthy and can create happiness and peace. Standing on the 'what ifs' and 'should have/could haves' is not healthy for us. The "Maybe I should have checked on them," or "If only I had been there," "Maybe I should have done this or that," or "Maybe it's my fault."

It is time to renew, release, and let go. Yesterday is gone. There is nothing you can do to bring them back. You can't "should've" done something. You can only *DO* something. Renew yourself. Release that attachment.

"Today is a new day!" as Steve Maraboli said.

There are many negative thoughts that are not good to keep believing around the death of our loved ones. I know. I have interviewed many of you still holding onto those things that do not serve your amazing life now. It is time to let go and forgive yourself or even someone else around the death. We must unlearn what we have been programmed to believe about ourselves since we were young. This programming really *no longer* serves you.

Steve Maraboli also said, "The truth is, unless you let go, unless you forgive yourself, unless you forgive the situation, unless you realize that the situation is over, you cannot move forward."

In order to move on and find peace and be whole, we have to dump the rocks (our stuff) we have purposely picked up. We have to let it go. I often will write and burn. Write letters to people who have hurt me (*do not* send them), write letters to myself or the ones gone. I usually always burn them.

It doesn't serve anyone to send the letters.

It took me fourteen years to the date to realize I was carrying around huge rocks in my backpack. It was fourteen years after she had died to find whole peace in Ariann's death. Thirteen heartache Christmases, birthdays, and Mother's Days. Thirteen-plus years of torturing myself, remembering my own guilt, and combining it with the pains of words said to me by others that I believed.

One glorious day, through some serious personal development courses I was taking, I realized I blamed myself for not being good enough to be her mom, and for being that bad girl, that rebellious teenager who felt like I did not deserve her—she was too perfect for me. I felt like God was punishing me for my sins.

Remember the moment I said, "I don't deserve her," when she was born and then when she died, I declared, "I deserved that!"? What crazy stuff that was.

That's not how life works. I realized in one beautiful moment that *that* was complete nonsense I was carrying around. In that gracious space, a week before Christmas, I said, "*Enough*! THIS IS DONE!" I would not allow it to plague me anymore. I was her mother. I was so very blessed to be her mother. She chose me to be her mother and I chose her to be my angel daughter. I would chose her again.

God blessed me with her for four months physically and forever spiritually. I was going to take that gift and hold on tight to it. Forever.

I was able to completely stomp out the crazy, guilty notions I had carried with me since her birth and death. In that moment, I stood in my power and accepted it exactly as it was. Dumping anything else that did not serve me. Emptying my backpack right there. There was nothing I could have/should have done. It was what it was. I was done believing the lies and anything else that was not good and did not serve me around her death. I was finished with it. No more.

C. JoyBell C. said, "You will find it is necessary to let things go; simply for the reason they are heavy. So let them go, let go of them. I tie no weights to my ankles."

...or, put them in my backpack. It's probably time for you to dump some items, too. If you're using this book as a personal development book, it's time to go write and see what comes up for you, now.

At my personal development course that night, people kept saying, "Wow, you are glowing."

And I said, "Yep, I unleashed an angel tonight."

I felt her glowing in and all around me. I believe we are so closely connected with the sweet souls we physically lose. Imagine the heartaches they feel knowing we are torturing ourselves around their deaths and telling ourselves the lies. Being told the untruths, too. They are totally aware of our pains and heartaches—the comments being made to us and the words we say to ourselves. It must be truly difficult for them to move on and be happy in their new mission because of us tightly holding on to them in our earthly agony.

I believe she felt that from me. It was like I had a chain on her and I had been chaining her down with my baggage—my large piece of luggage I hauled around with lots of past crap.

As I let it all go that weekend, I felt her soar. I felt her fly. I freed her. Truly.

C. JoyBell C. said,
A star falls from the sky and into your hands. Then it seeps through your veins and swims inside your blood and becomes every part of you. And then you have to put it back into the sky. And it's the most painful thing you'll ever have to do and that you've ever done. But what's yours is yours. Whether it's up in the sky or here in your hands. And one day, it'll fall from the sky and hit you in the head real hard and that time, you won't have to put it back in the sky again.

I so look forward to that day.

Listen to the words of the beautiful Celine Dion song, *Fly*.

I felt this energy in me and around me shift so hugely from my letting go of my baggage around her. I felt her so immensely happy over the choice I made in letting go of that past stuff and being able to move forward.

I felt I had unleashed her and let her fly.

She lit me up that night. And flew again.

"Fly, precious one."

Stay tuned for more on this.

Journaling Thoughts

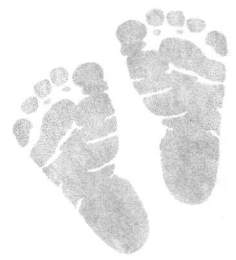

* 18 *

Finding your Purpose

"Every man and woman who serves the Lord, no matter how faithful they may be, have their dark hours; but if they have lived faithfully, light will burst upon them and relief will be furnished." ~Lorenzo Snow

That quote is a promise I hold on to. *Light bursting upon me and relief being furnished.* That sounds super great. There comes a time in our lives, even after loss when we start asking, "Now what? Now what does my life expect of me? What do I do with what I have been given? Can I make a difference even if I am still in the grief and on the crazy ride?"

Yes! Yes you can. I call it the sixth step of grief—Finding your purpose. Your *why* to go on.

In the beginning of 2020, I met a dynamic women whom I had lunch with. She shared her story of losing her teenage daughter to suicide and not wanting to live after that heartache. I could not even imagine that pain.

Through her grief ride, she told me she found God. She said what turned it for her, "was realizing I had a life to live and that I never wanted anyone else to go through this pain." She has become a powerful voice for her daughter and speaks God, love, and life into souls in pain, especially those who have lost to suicide.

She inspired me to step up and play bigger in my life. We are still here, no matter what has happened, to live, to grow, to learn, to love, to give, to serve and to be the best we can be. We still have a life to live and to live at the fullest we can with them guiding us.

Here's what we need to know: grieving and living go together in this next chapter of our life. Our 'new' life, now. We reconnect with our new life after loss, one step, one moment, one day at a time.

As we start to step back into our new lives, we are sometimes being driven by compassion and serving others. One of my first thoughts was to not want anyone else to experience the pain and heartache of SIDS. I became a SIDS donor, fundraiser for research, and a SIDS educator. I was teaching basic training to EMTs, First Responders, and educating in schools with Ariann's story. I also reached out and touched families who had experienced and were living the hell of their own recent losses. I became president of the local SIDS support group and facilitated healing that way, not just for them but for me, as well.

This helped me in finding heart and compassion in giving back to others. Service. A little bit of life serving and doing good after my big loss made a HUGE difference for me. It had me see other's dealing with their own pain and heartache and wanting to make a difference—to help them.

Dieter F. Uchtdorf said, "As we lose ourselves in the service of others we discover our own lives and our own happiness."

I feel like a huge part of finding purpose is to slowly step back in to things in our new life that need the most attention. After my baby died, I began to organize our stuff from a move we made right after her death. To create a home we were ready to fully *live* in.

To then look into where we can serve as we learn to be with the grief and pain of loss.

We can ask ourselves, "Are there important activities we cut out after the loss? Activities that meant something?"

Maybe it's time to schedule these back in—hobbies we loved and filled us with joy. Even if it feels like effort, it's probably a good time to step back in to them.

What other positive and therapeutic actions could we take or have we wanted to take? It might be a good time to start an exercise class, an art project, or even something that would honor the memory of our loved one. It might be time to schedule activities in our day, in the week, or even sometime in the coming months.

I am a true believer in accountability partners from my tribe and in our business life. It might be a good time to ask someone to be that for you—to keep you accountable for doing what you feel would be good in moving in the direction of your new life every day.

I used my accountability partner to keep me accountable to taking a long walk once the first week, two times the next, three times the next week. She kept me accountable to find one thing that brought me joy in the week and doing it. To find one thing to have fun around and to laugh at, and not feeling guilty about it. To find one thing in giving myself some self-care/self-love time.

She was there to listen to me in any moment of the journey, yet she was also there to push me to say, "It's okay to start living again."

Who can this be for you as you also step into your *purposeful* life?

Mahatma Gandhi said, "The best way to find yourself is to lose yourself in the service of others."

As the years go by, we start to be driven by compassion and the need to help others. Service and compassion become the driver as fear and despair sit in the back of our car. They are still there in the background—they're just not driving anymore. Compassion for others and compassion for ourselves is where we're heading. If we choose to be courageous, despite being sad, heartbroken, upset and afraid, we step in to our life in the new way it'll go. A new path to follow.

It might be a good time for us to make dinner for our family and some extra for our neighbor who is lonely and has no family close by. Or someone who is sick and in need of a home-cooked or yummy store-bought soup. It's when we give money to the man living on the streets. It's when we start to listen to others' stories and become a healer for them. Because you now know. You have felt the hopelessness, and you have some hope to give.

In Matthew 25:35-40, the Savior shares the beautiful story of taking care of others, which is truly taking care of Him.

> *For I was hungry and you gave me something to eat, I was thirsty and you gave me something to drink, I was a stranger and you invited me in, I needed clothes and you clothed me, I was sick and you looked after me, I was in prison and you came to visit me.*
>
> *Then the righteous will answer him, 'Lord, when did we see you hungry and feed you, or thirsty and give you something to drink? When did we see you a stranger and invite you in, or needing clothes and clothe you? When did we see you sick or in prison and go to visit you?'*

> *The King will reply, 'Truly I tell you, whatever you did for one of the least of these brothers and sisters of mine, you did for me..'*

"There is nothing small in the service of God." Saint Francis De Sales said. It's the stage when grief and fear no longer tell you what you should do and not do. You're finally driven by doing good because you *know* how it feels to be afraid, sad, and all alone. It's how I found my way to you.

Let me tell you about my family and their *great service* in our community. The day after my little sister, Becca died, we as a family had all gathered in our restaurant's conference room to talk and mourn her life—which was suddenly gone from this earth.

We were at our restaurant and yet we were not eating, funny how that was. Within a few hours, tables were filled with food from friends and neighbors to love on us. We saw the importance of food, especially at a time like that. It truly meant so very much to us. Ever since then, my parents and my brother reach out to the community to love on those who have lost to death. They have had a huge impact on feeding thousands at times of grief, heartache, and hopelessness.

To also bear testimony that "this, too, shall slowly pass and purpose will come again."

Our family learned to serve and feed other families because of the service given to us at the time of our deepest despair. My family watches for the deaths in the community and reaches out to the family to let that family know my family will be feeding them in the next week. It mostly happens around the viewing/funeral.

The Cottam family from *Bella's Fresh Mexican Grill*, Farr West, Utah is known for miles and miles for their service and love in the community at hard times. That's what finding your purpose is about around the loss of someone—you realizing you can still make a difference, and you can leave your loved one's name on a mark in this world.

There is a beautiful story of a family who also lost their little boy, Nolan to SIDS. In his memory, they started ACTS of Kindness for Nolan. Every year on his birthday and weeks after, they do random acts of kindness in his name with a card that says, RANDOM ACTS OF LOVE IN HONOR OF NOLAN.

It's a way of remembering him in their hearts and moving forward after their loss.

I also contribute to the Aaron Matthew SIDS Research Guild, named after John and Heather Kahan's son who died of SIDS shortly after his birth. It was established to fund much-needed research in the field at Seattle Children's Hospital Integrative Brain Research Institute (Seattle Children's). That was finding a new purpose because of and through grief and the loss.

There is life after. It is a good life if we chose it to be. Looking at what inspires us, even from the particulars around our loved one's death, could be the life after for a time. I am no longer involved in the SIDS organization. Yet, it was what helped me move on in my life and find ways of giving back that inspired me. Which then continued and continued as I kept moving forward. The ways we find of honoring the ones we love and buried are positive to have us step in to our life again—finding our new *purpose*.

Did our loved ones have final wishes or did we see a need in the past few months of their lives? Is it time to ask yourself, "What does my day look like if I involve myself here? What did it look like before? What could it look like now?"

After the passing of my husband's mom, we saw a need with some of her friends and people she loved. We reached out and have continued to support and make a difference for them. It eases the hole in our hearts, a tiny bit. In her memory.

In their memory, what can you do?

It might be time to make a plan. What activities were a part of your day that were important or of value to you? Is it time to schedule a few of those back in? Even if it doesn't feel joyful to you? I get it, not much might right now. Yet, it would be good to get some things in your day to create your life as you know it now.

Making a plan is always good, but with no action, a plan is just a plan. What can you schedule into your day, or your week that would have you step into your inspired plan? Maybe an earlier rise with a walk or a hike to just think about what you could do to *Find Your Purpose* again.

Your passion can become your purpose. You were created for something awesome through that and because of that—find that purpose!

Viktor E. Frankl was a highly respected psychiatrist in his native Austria, when he was transported to Auschwitz in 1944. Against all odds, Frankl survived concentration camp. After his liberation, and having lost his wife and his family through it all, he wrote, *Man's Search for Meaning* about his experience in the death camps.

Viktor explain the prisoners' situation saying, "He who has a *why* to live for can bear almost any *how*."

Frankl came to understand he needed to stop expecting something better from life, and instead ask himself ,"What life expects from me." In other words, he believed he owed it to life—to the fact he had been born and, despite it all, was still on the Earth—to make himself the best person possible.

He wrote, "The ultimate meaning of life can be found by taking responsibility for one's actions and making use of opportunities to better oneself."

He said, "When we are no longer able to change a situation, we are challenged to change ourselves."

Can we have this life attitude, no matter what happens?

Time to hear Louise Armstrong's *What a Wonderful World*.

It *is* a Wonderful World. I hope you can step into it, leaving it better for what you have learned.

Journaling Thoughts

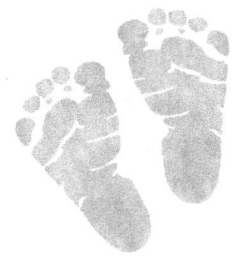

* 19 *

God's Plan vs. My Plan

"We search for happiness. We long for peace. We hope for love. And the Lord showers us with an amazing abundance of blessings. But intermingled with the joy and happiness, one thing is certain: there will be moments, hours, days, sometimes years when your soul will be wounded." ~ Neil L. Andersen

I WAS BORN OF GOODLY PARENTS. I was born to good Christian parents, who took it literally when God said, "Multiply and replenish the earth." My parents had ten kids. And then, because that was not enough for their big, loving hearts, they adopted a Navajo girl from New Mexico when she was six—whom we love and adore.

My parents raised us to be good Christians. My mom had all eleven of us at church by 9:05AM in the second pew of the chapel every Sunday. I do not know how she did it, but she deserves sainthood for doing so. My dad had us up every morning at 5:30AM reading the scriptures.

Sunday night *Disney*, weekly family nights, and family vacations were a must growing up in our home. We were taught and learned the Gospel of Jesus Christ in our very humble, impoverished home environment. I went to church and Sunday school weekly, learning to be Christ-like, giving all, and to live a happy, fulfilling life.

Despite my own difficult childhood and teenage years, I had a good upbringing. Being raised in that and in the teachings of Christ, no one ever said, "You grow up and get married and then babies die, and life is difficult and you might get divorced and raise another baby as a single mom."

No one ever talked about their trials or hard times—or I didn't hear that mentioned, so I guess I felt like it wasn't part of life. Why was I so disillusioned? Why did I not see life could/would be any different than happy?

I know it is not something said in Sunday school or even in a Young Women's Church class. How could they know to tell us that? Yet, I didn't ever even hear the adults in my life talk about their struggles, their challenges, their hard times as they taught and educated me. I just never heard the hard of life from the adults in my life growing up.

I understand and get it, because years ago, when my daughter came home after an upset with her husband, she said to me, "Why didn't you tell me marriage was hard?"

I laughed, as I had been divorced three times and even though I was in my final eternal marriage, I guess I did not verbally tell her marriage was hard. I thought she watched my life and would get it.

Despite that, through all of growing up, I never heard it and I never got it. I heard them talk about walking with God and trusting in God. But also at my time of hard, I didn't get the 'trust in God' and 'know that He has a plan' even in hard times.

I had this fairytale idea of once you choose God's plan, *it all works out happily ever after*. I had the thought of when and if I really did turn to God, all was going to work out for me. *My* way, of course.

Quentin L. Cook says, "Life is not easy, nor was it meant to be."

Hmmmmm? Wish I would've heard that when I was in my teens, but *would* I have heard it?

Elder Cook also says, "Think of the Savior in the Garden of Gethsemane as He is suffering. He knows the hard we are having. He knows and has felt it for us. He is there with us and He is walking that hard time right there with us."

I *now*, many years later, *know* it to be truth. Despite me, my Heavenly Father and Savior, Jesus Christ were with me through the pain and heartache of burying Ariann and even beyond.

As a twenty year old, I finally *did* accept my Father in Heaven and the Gospel of Jesus Christ into my life. I was going to church and teaching Sunday school to thirteen-year-olds. I did step into my faith whole-heartedly...or so I thought.

Yet, when that Christmas morning came and we woke up and the joy of our lives was gone, it was a *hard hit*. *My* "reason for the season" disappearing on Christmas morning was a harsh punch in the gut.

When Ariann died, I was angry. *Very* angry. I felt betrayed by the adults in my life for not telling me about the reality of life. Harshly and mostly, I was angry with God. Why would He do this to me? Why was He punishing me? She was my perfect, beautiful angel. Why would He take her from me?

Was I guilty because I was a bad girl when I was young? Did I bring this punishment on me? Was it really because I didn't breast feed? Was it partly or all my fault?

So many times, those are the question that we ask. *Why did this happen? Was I at fault? Were they at fault? Why do I need this hard thing? What did I do or not do?! Were they or I in the wrong place or wrong time?*

There is definitely an inequality or unfairness in this life that is very confusing to us human beings when death or intense trials happen. *What did I do to deserve this? Why did this happen to me?* These are questions asked a lot in losing someone close, someone we love. Those are questions I asked a lot.

Those are not the right questions to be asking.

Richard R. Scott said,

> *When you face adversity, you can be led to ask many questions. Some serve a useful purpose; others do not. To ask, why does this have to happen to me? Why do I have to suffer this, now? What have I done to cause this? These questions will lead you into blind alleys. It really does no good to ask questions that reflect opposition to the will of God. Rather ask, what am I to do? What am I to learn from this experience? What am I to change? Whom am I to help? How can I remember my many blessings in times of trial? Willing sacrifice of deeply held personal desires in favor of the will of God is very hard to do. Yet, when you pray with real conviction, "Please let me know Thy will," and "May Thy will be done," you are in the strongest position to receive the maximum help from your loving Father.*

What am I to learn from this experience? What am I to change? Who am I to help? How can I remember my many blessings in time of trial?

I love the story of the Savior healing the blind man in John Chapter 9,

> *And as Jesus passed by, he saw a man which was blind from his birth. And his disciples asked him, saying, 'Master, who did sin, this man, or his parents, that he was born blind?' Jesus answered, 'Neither hath this*

man sinned, nor his parents: but that the works of God should be made manifest in Him. I must work the works of him that sent me, while it is day: the night cometh, when no man can work. As long as I am in the world, I am the light of the world.'

That the works of God should be made manifest in Him. Events happen so God can do his work. So His plan can be fulfilled. Not our plan. HIS. Looking to Christ we are able to see, even the things we don't want to see.

On another occasion, Jesus came upon a group arguing vehemently with His disciples. When the Savior inquired as to the cause of the contention, the father of an afflicted child stepped forward, saying he had approached Jesus's disciples for a blessing for his son, but they were not able to provide it.

With the boy still gnashing his teeth, foaming from the mouth, and thrashing on the ground in front of them, the father appealed to Jesus with what must have been last-resort desperation in his voice:

"If thou canst do anything," he said, "have compassion on us, and help us."

Jesus said unto him, "If thou canst believe, all things are possible to him that believeth."

And straightway the father of the child cried out, and said with tears, "Lord, I believe; help thou mine unbelief."

This man's initial conviction, by his own admission, was limited. But he had an urgent, emphatic desire in behalf of his only child. We are told it was good enough for a beginning.

"Even if ye can no more than desire to believe," Alma declares, "let this desire work in you, even until ye believe."

God does not always act the way we humans would act, but He does always act in a way that is ultimately for our good. When we step in to Him, believing in Him.

"For as the heavens are higher than the earth, so are my ways higher than your ways and my thoughts than your thoughts." (Isaiah 55:9)

What if that *was* God's plan? What if that was his way of revealing his plan and it has nothing to do with what you did or didn't do, but because it's God's plan—it is the way it is. His will. His way.

One of the most favorite and the most popular stories of the *Old Testament* is the story of Joseph and his coat of many colors. He was his dad's favorite and his brothers were super jealous of that. Starting in Genesis 37, as a seventeen-year-old kid his brothers took him, threw him into a pit, threatened to take his life but then sold him as a slave to spice traders who took him into Egypt.

Everything he knew and loved was taken from him at a young age. He was separated from his family for decades, made to be a slave, hit on by his boss's wife and then wrongly accused despite his innocence, imprisoned and left in prison even though he was a man of integrity, honesty, hard work ...and *Innocent*.

He was given the gift of interpreter dreams by God and followed the will of God. He made a difference for Egypt by letting them know a famine was coming and they needed to be prepared. Pharaoh made him ruler over Egypt in preparations.

Returning to his story in Chapter 45, his brothers came into Egypt to gather food for the family. Joseph put them through a series of tests to prove they had changed. Then, he finally told them who he was. They were so apologetic and bowed down before him.

Joseph says in v. 7, "and God sent me" and in v. 8, "So now it was not you that sent me hither, BUT GOD; and he hath made me a father to Pharaoh and a Lord of all his house, and a ruler throughout all the land of Egypt."

And then in Genesis 50:20, Joseph says, "You intended to harm me, but God intended it for good to accomplish what is now being done, the saving of many lives."

After all of it, Joseph could say his brothers "intended to harm [him], BUT GOD intended it for good to accomplish what is now being done, the saving of many lives."

That, of course, didn't dawn on Joseph as a seventeen-year old who would've been praying for deliverance out of the pit, for deliverance out of the spice traders' hands, for deliverance out of Pharaohs wife's hands, for deliverance out of the prison BUT GOD...

This is a guiding principle—BUT GOD, no matter the circumstances, God holds the ending.

Here is a fun research in the Bible. Go and find how many BUT GOD scriptures there are. I will tell you there are upper thirty of them.

Genesis 8:1—"But God remembered Noah and all the wild animals and the livestock that were with him in the ark, and He sent a wind over the earth, and the waters receded."

Psalm 73:26—"My flesh and my heart may fail, but God is the strength of my heart and my portion forever."

Matthew 19:26—"Jesus looked at them and said, 'With man this is impossible, but with God all things are possible.'"

What if you were to take negative thoughts around your loss or what you're dealing with and be encouraged by adding, BUT GOD? I am discouraged, BUT GOD encourages. I am lonely, BUT GOD comforts. BUT GOD has a plan. BUT GOD KNOWS ALL!

Nothing I did or didn't do would've made a difference. That was the works of God, and so is whatever we are dealing with.

"There are no accidents," as my parents said and as I now say. That's exactly as it was supposed to be with God. Even because of *choices*. It is God's way in all things. Because of God's Holy Plan, we know that birth and death are actually just milestones on our journey to eternal life with our Heavenly Father. Death is a necessary transition, but it is not the *final* transition. It is just a temporary one. One that we as human beings don't quite comprehend when it happens.

We must ask ourselves, "What am I to learn from this experience? What am I to change? Who am I to help? How can I remember my many blessings in time of trial?"

To ask the questions, "How can I have an eternal perspective on this death or this trial? How can I see through this into eternity?" is looking to see into God's will and His way as Joseph did with his brothers.

My dad knew and quickly testified of this eternal perspective when my sweet baby, his grand-baby, died and then again when his own baby girl died. He knew. He knew what the plan was and he knew where they were. He testified that knowledge to many after the death of my baby sister. My dad knew that, held on to it, and still does.

There is no end when it comes to death. "Only what's next for them on their mission," as my dad says.

> *The 'lively hope' we are given by the resurrection of Jesus Christ is our conviction that death is not the conclusion of our identity but merely a necessary step in the destined transition from mortality to immortality. This hope changes the whole perspective of mortal life. The assurance of resurrection and immortality affects how we look on the physical challenges of mortality, how we live our mortal lives, and how we relate to those around us. ~ Dallin H. Oaks*

I tell you honesty, I really struggled with God's plan for a very long time. It took me many years pulled back and away from the Gospel and God to actually feel God stirring in me. My parents were amazing grandparents taking my other daughter, Emalee to church and primary and giving her a good basis of the gospel in her life. I so did not.

As Emalee was turning eight, it was a surprise to me people asked if I was going to have her baptized and come unto Jesus Christ. I had not even thought about it. Of course, that would be a good question to ask me. Why would or wouldn't I have her baptized into The Church of Jesus Christ of Latter Day Saints—the Gospel I knew and was brought up in?

I was born, raised, and lived in Utah most of my life at this point. I remember saying, "Maybe out of Utah, I would go to church."

When Emalee, at eight years old took the missionary lessons, for the first time in forever I felt the Spirit strongly around me. She was baptized, by her choice, and I felt the Spirit even more so stirring in me. But I also felt the guilt and still quite a bit of anger with God and His plan.

A few months after Emalee was baptized, the husband I was married to at the time was transferred to California. We moved to a darling area outside of Fresno, called Madera Ranchos. We loved it there.

My first Saturday night there, the Spirit of God whispered to me saying, "I put you here as you asked, now are you going to church tomorrow?"

"Yes! Yes, I am."

I found the local Church of Jesus Christ of Latter Day Saints in Madera and walked myself into it the very next day—my first Sunday in California.

It was a peaceful and powerful moment of feeling God's hands in my life turning me to Him. Through continually turning to Him, I began to gain a solid testimony of His Will, His Way, and His Light. He was and is so mindful of me, despite me. I testify of this.

He knows *all*. He guides *all*. He only wants us to turn to Him, no matter what we are feeling, angry, upset, hurt, or lost. He is still with us and ready for us to be with Him during our hard times.

There is an amazing book called *Left to Tell: Discovering God Amidst the Rwandan Holocaust*. The author, Immaculee Ilibagiza shares her powerful story. She is a survivor of the Rwanda, Africa genocide, where she survived by living in a tiny bathroom with seven others for a few months. Her story is exceptional and a must-read.

In her book, she said something really profound that related to me and my journey. She wrote:

> *I came to learn that God never shows us something we aren't ready to understand. Instead, He lets us see what we need to see, when we need to see it. He'll wait until our eyes and hearts are open to Him, and then when we're ready, He will plant our feet on the path that's best for us...but it's up to us to do the walking.*

I feel that to be true for me. He waited for me, in my time, in my space. When I was ready, He was still there loving me all through it. What an amazing God He is.

In John 16:33, the Savior spoke this truth, "These things I have spoken to you, that in me ye might have peace. In the world ye shall have tribulation: but be of good cheer: I have overcome the world."

Proverbs 3:5 says, "Trust in the Lord with all thine heart; and lean not unto thine own understanding."

Trusting in Him in peace and trusting that joy comes after sorrow is also His will. That will be the great leap we need to thrive in our life's tribulations. I was grateful to finally have been given a tiny perspective of how to step in to God instead of away from Him. I found immense peace in my own personal suffering. Joy did come after such a great sorrow.

One of my favorite quotes in times of life's hard stuff says,

Don't you quit! You keep walking. You keep trying. There is help and happiness ahead. Some blessings come soon, some come late, and some don't come until heaven; but for those who embrace the gospel of Jesus Christ, they come. It will be all right in the end. Trust God and believe in good things to come. ~ Jeffrey R. Holland

That sums it up, right? Not so easy in the midst of your grief and heartache. Yet, quite accurate. There is a saying in my business that you can only quit on a good day. Which is really never, right?

Jeffrey R. Holland also says, "When life is hard, remember—we are not the first to ask, 'Is there no other way?'"

There is no other way. It's the way we are to go. Thinking of that, I step in to trusting Him and create my own affirmation around Him every day.

I say, "Everything always works out for my higher good." Trusting Him, I know everything always works out.

I also love to sing the part of Oklahoma song that says, "Everything's going my way."

Putting our trust in God, we know everything will go our way. Honoring His will is trusting Him and not thinking we know, or thinking it should be a different way.

Gordon B Hinckley said, "It is not as bad as you sometimes think it is. It all works out, don't worry. If you do your best, it will all work out. Put your trust in God and move forward with Faith."

I know that sounds difficult in the midst of your hard. I am sorry, I know. Beyond the moment we are in, it, too, will pass. It will work out. We will find peace. God knows and loves all involved. If we are believers, we must step forward in faith, trusting in Him as He has asked us to. Just like my own father did when he lost his daughter.

Hillary Scott sings the beautiful Christian song, *Thy Will*... I leave the QRC for you now. Scan and listen to this beautiful song.

His will be done in *all* we do. I pray we may find this path to walk.

Just remember, "The Lord compensates the faithful for every loss... Every tear today will eventually be returned a hundredfold with tears of rejoicing and gratitude." Joseph B. Wirthlin

Doesn't that sound *amazing*?

A hundredfold with tears of rejoicing and gratitude.

Ahhhhhhh—I look forward to that.

JOURNALING THOUGHTS

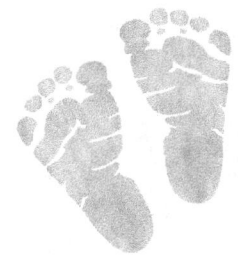

* 20 *

God Moments

"God never leaves us alone, never leaves us unaided in the challenges that we face." Jeffrey R. Holland

I TRULY BELIEVE IN THESE SIMPLE words. I might not have believed this years ago when my baby died, but today I firmly believe He never leaves us alone. He did not leave me. He has not and will not leave you. The 'Grace of God' or the moments I like to call "God Moments" are moments we get to see God's powerful hand in our life. I *believe* He gives us God moments to remind us He is there. It could be a simple and seemly coincidental moment but also could be a profound, serendipitous, and miraculous moment. They are like a super power, these God moments. I honor and enjoy these moments when they come. I love to count them at the end of the day. Don't discount them. There are no accidents, only what is meant to be.

Dr. Joe Dispenza says, "Is that odd, or is that God?" That's God!

I would ask you… Are you seeking for these God moments? Are you asking for the simple ways of His hand to be shown daily as you grieve? Are you hoping and praying for him to appear in monumental, life-altering ways? Are you asking Him to send your angel to comfort and show you His will?

Are you seeking for God moments in every moment of your days?

There are so many ways of having these tender moments grace us and being reminded God knows us, and our loved ones are with us.

In early March of 2020, we buried my mother-in-law. She was sick from cancer for a few years and slowly going down. We saw so many God moments as she was passing—to the morning she passed as well as after, into the burial week and still beyond. He gave us those moments to remind us He is still in charge and He is still mindful of us.

Just recently, a hummingbird flitted around me, reminding me Mom was still with us.

One of the greatest lessons I read in the beautiful book, *The Message* by Lance Richardson, was, "The greatest mission of those who pass, is ministering and guiding the ones on earth who have been left behind."

That's you and me. Our loved ones are with us and do become our hummingbirds, frogs, feathers, the wind—our guardian angels, whispering to us and in many ways reminding us they are with us. Our Angels bringing those God moments. That's their new mission.

I believe, after many years of spiritual experiences around this, there are many ways we will see, feel, and know our loved ones are in our lives. There are many ways we'll be reminded they are around and so super close to us. You'll have thoughts and feelings around them.

Numbers will show up. Rainbows appear. The wind whispers to us. Sunsets rock our world. Electricity plays a nutty part. Animals and insects tend to happen in many God moments. Objects in our paths appear. Very real and distinctive dreams. Fragrances and smells that remind us of them. Feelings of being watched, looked upon. Buzzing in our ears. Music at exactly the right time needed for me at the exact moment I needed.

These are all God moments. Or 'Angels are watching over me,' as I say. I believe the beautiful scripture, "Be Still and Know that I am God," reminds us to be still and listen, watch, and let His hand show up when it shows up. Let the God moments happen as they may. Acknowledge them as they are.

On the morning of the death of my husband's mom, his nephew stepped onto the back porch for a breath of fresh air and a hummingbird flew right up to him, fluttering around his face. He is not a believer, yet he *knew* it was his grandma reminding him she was still with him even though she had passed. She loved hummingbirds in her back yard. God moment. So quickly after she passed, she shows right back up.

Please do not be like me, sitting around expecting the signs and the God moments, because they won't show, I promise you. It's only when you step back, not attached and let God's hand work in His time and His way that you experience His tender mercies. Be still and watch.

As you see and think of the animals, insects, objects, smells, dreams that show up, remember—God moments.

A few months or so after Ariann passed away, I went up to my favorite place in the world, Zion's National park in Southern Utah and hiked Angels Landing.

Angels Landing, known previously as the Temple of Aeolus, is a 1,488-foot-tall rock formation in Zion National Park in southwestern Utah, United States. A trail cut into solid rock in 1926 leads to the top of Angels Landing and provides a whole view of Zion Canyon. It is breathtaking and one of the most beautiful places in the world.

As I hiked this amazing trail of Angels Landing, where Ariann's dad and I met a few years earlier, a glorious big white butterfly landed right on me and then flitted in and out around me. It was stunningly white, very large and it stuck with me for a good hour or more. It was the first time after her death that I felt the sweet energy of Ari hanging with me. I was so grateful for that God moment. I have had so many more with butterflies since then.

I have heard countless stories of "signs" showing up this way after their loved ones pass. Dragonflies, hummingbirds, frogs, and many more of God's creatures become a part of our tender God moments in knowing our loved ones are close. Here is what I believe: they are *always with us* and we are their greatest mission.

Helen Keller said it perfectly, "What we once enjoyed and deeply loved we can never lose, for all we love deeply becomes part of us."

I believe our Heavenly Father is so mindful of us and our need to be comforted. It's one way He uses to comfort us. By letting them be there with us and for us.

Unfortunately, it's a sign some people might ignore. I surely hope not. Our loved ones may try to communicate with us in every unimaginable manner. By using these ways, they're sending us a message without trying to scare us. They're letting us know, *I'm with you. You're not alone. Keep going.*

Right after her father's funeral, one of my good friends was having a hard and a sad moment. As she was standing out on a patio looking over a lake, she had a hummingbird in her face—bopping up and down for quite a few minutes. She felt it was a beautiful message from her dad, he was with her.

In 2017-2018, we were in Ethiopia on a LDS Church Mission. During one part, I was having a really hard time. I felt like I was on a difficult mission in that country, and I had a lot going on physically with me. One Saturday, as we cleaned the church, I was up front dusting the pulpit and all of a sudden, a tiny little tree frog jumped out of from under the pulpit and landed on the wall.

I was in awe of, 'How in the world did it get in?' Was that odd, or was that God? I knew it was a sweet moment of Rebecca in my hard time. Frogs were Rebecca's *favorite* thing ever. She collected all things frogs. Frogs were our family's reminder Rebecca was close. It was a tender mercy moment for me, as I was reminded God knows me, He knew where I was and He *knew* exactly what I needed—a tiny frog in the front of a locked-up chapel to remind me I am watched over and loved on.

The one sweet memory of that dreadful Christmas morning I had many years ago, when my baby died, was waking up at 2:33 AM and wondering why was I awake? I wasn't sure why I was awake right at that exact time. I had felt something unusual but was unsure and did not recognize what it was until years later. I realized with inspiration that this was her moment of saying goodbye as she passed on. I often wake up at 2:33 AM. I feel the closest to my baby and my Father in Heaven at that time. I am reminded that God's hand is in all things in our lives.

Interesting...as right at this moment of writing, I look over at the clock on the side of the bed and it's displaying 5:55 AM. When this happens, I always say, "Angels are watching over me and everything always works out."

I believe God's hand allows us to see these signs, including numbers, animals, and music to remind us. Signs are given so that we may believe in Him, Jesus Christ. These are to remind us of hope, that we are on the right path, and to keep on going. These God moments bring us peace and comfort in our times of great loss. Numbers are a great sign of The Lord and His tender mercy showing us the way. So as 5:55 popped up, I question the meaning of it.

The meaning of 555: "You are aligning with higher consciousness. By seeing 555, *'the angels want you to know everything is for your highest good and you are slowly coming into alignment with higher consciousness.'* This will raise your vibration, enabling you to help and heal those around you." (Interesting because this is a healing book.)

Most importantly we need to pay attention to our intuition—our inner voice—the Holy Spirit for guidance, and to prepare us for a new phase in our life.

It was a cool moment for me, to be reminded that, 'Everything happens for a reason, and the higher purpose of all things come to pass as we are guided in every moment. When you see numbers and see them often—usually by the third time seeing the same ones, it might be time to think it's a precious God moment for you. The numbers could be a birthday, an anniversary, the date of their passing, the time of their passing, or even repeating numbers such as 111, 222, 333, etc. These numbers may appear on clocks, billboards, phone numbers, or any other familiar place. They can also come from family, friends, or even strangers.

Seeing repetitive triple number patterns, like 222 or 1234 is not a coincidence. Repetitive numbers is a form of synchronicity and its God's way of telling you that you are in sync with your true self—the real you—and you are in sync with the angels in your life. You are aligned on the path He has for you.

A friend recently was in my home. I have a clock stuck on 7:11. She told me that was her granddad's favorite number, reminding her he is with her again and again.

If you start seeing a pattern and believe your loved one is communicating with you, take comfort in knowing they are with you. I believe you should just *know* that is a moment God wants you to have to comfort and that He is guiding you. Grab a little book and start documenting the things you are seeing, hearing, and opening to as you step in to angels among us.

My daughter and I (quite a few months ago) starting texting each other every time we saw, 11:11 or 12:12 or 1:11 or 2:22 or 3:33 and so on. It has been fun throughout the day watching these numbers pop up for one or both of us. Remind yourself of this in every moment you see a small sign of God's goodness showing. I see them every day.

I challenge you to step into discovering the unexpected beauty of God's hands in the ordinary of life including in the midst of grief. Find the God moments. Expect them to show. Be still and know that He is. In those moments, we get to have the gifts of being reminded of the Ultimate Love of God.

Are there really angels among us? I believe so. They know how to communicate and guide us in ways our minds might not understand. They know us and they want to communicate with us. I believe they show up in so many ways.

I have a friend who has stood at the bedsides of many people as they passed from this life. She has had countless experiences that have strengthened her knowledge our loved ones are in many ways as present with us after death as they are during life. We cannot typically see them, but they are often there to help us through our various challenges—including our grief over their passing.

Ezra Taft Benson taught, "Sometimes the veil between this life and the life beyond becomes very thin. Our loved ones who have passed on are not far from us."

One of the songs that bore testimony to me on this topic was the group Alabama, singing, *Angels Among Us*. It was written by a woman, Becky Hobbs, who had a crazy premonition of dying and one day had a voice say to her, "Be careful as this could be your last birthday."

She then had a life-changing experience with her band where they were hit by a truck. All of them walked away from it, when they shouldn't have. She then wrote that beautiful song,

Angels show up when needed or when it's time to show us something in God's eye, I truly believe. Angels are among us. All around us. To guide us. To comfort us and to show us the way. Even in this life as other human beings make a difference for us.

Angels Among Us, sung by Alabama

I challenge you to watch for those God moments, or let's also call them Tender Mercies from Him who sees and knows all.

Journaling Thoughts

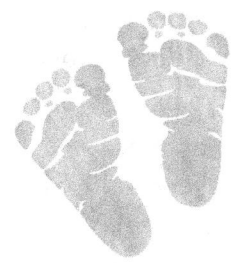

* 21 *

TENDER MERCIES from GOD

The Lord's tender mercies are very personal and individualized blessings, strength, protection, assurances, guidance, loving-kindnesses, consolation, support, and spiritual gifts which we receive from and because of and through the Lord Jesus Christ. Truly, the Lord suits "his mercies according to the conditions of the children of men." ~ Elder Bednar

THESE TENDER MERCIES ARE DEFINITELY gifts from God in all things and in all times, given to His children whom He loves unconditional. I know tender mercies are given to us to strengthen us when we do not have much strength to go on. To give us *Hope* even in times of no hope. They are given to all of us no matter, if we just hold tight in faith and hope, knowing He provides.

One of my sweetest tender mercies from God came fourteen years almost to the date of Ariann's death, after the personal development course in which I saw my rocks in my bags—the stuff I was holding onto. I let it all go and because of that, I stepped into her light and began to glow. Remember that story I shared in an earlier chapter?

After that education course, later that night, I was still up after helping my little sister, Rebecca make a quilt for her boyfriend. It was exactly one week before Christmas. I was then home alone, wrapping gifts to place under my Christmas tree.

It was the perfect setting with the holiday decor and the sweetness of the Christmas spirit. The only lights that were on in our tiny, little farm home were the lights of the large Christmas tree. It was 2:30AM and everything was still and oh, so peaceful.

I then felt the power of the Holy Spirit in the room. Probably quite like that first Christmas morning years and years ago when the Christ child was born. Then, in a precious, unpredictable moment, I felt the arms of an angel wrap around me. My angel. My sweet angel. She showed up.

Wow! Did she show up in a big way that night. Larger than life. Her arms and whole being wrapped so tightly around me and my whole body. I felt so much love. Such God love. Love like I had never felt before. My whole body and soul felt immersed in nothing but *Love*. Pure Eternal *Love*. Unconditional *Love*. Like I have never felt before.

With tears streaming down my face, I said, "Ariann, my sweet Ari girl. I love you so much."

And I felt her love for me. I felt her hug me so tight. I weeped in this tender mercy—this beautiful God moment a few days before Christmas. Fourteen years almost to the date of losing her, she returned to assure me that, 'Angels are watching over me and everything always works out.' Just trust and move forward.

For fourteen years, I had been waiting for her to show up like that. To tell me she was there. To give me some hope. To tell me it was okay.

It wasn't until I dumped the things that kept her and I disconnected, that finally allowed her to show up.

It was the briefest but most sweetest Christmas gift I have ever been given. I will always treasure that gift in my heart. A tender of all mercies. My Ariann moment for me, was to fully let it all go and powerfully move forward—letting her move forward. Given to me from God. In His time, in His way, because of my work and my faith. He gave freely. I am forever changed by this blessed God moment.

I share this with you, as sacred and tender as it is, for you to know it is available to all who step into God, trusting Him, hoping on Him, and letting go of the barriers between us and Him and our angels. Even after our trials and heartaches, He will provide. I promise you. Walk by faith asking for the tender mercies to show up.

We may falsely think such blessings and gifts are reserved for other people who appear to be more righteous or who serve or live better. I testify the tender mercies of the Lord are available to all of us and the Redeemer of Israel is eager to bestow such gifts upon each us. No matter what.

Three weeks after my Christmas healing—my beautiful Ariann God moment—on January 24th my sweet baby sister, Rebecca was killed in a car accident. My parents were in Hawaii on their vacation when it happened. That Monday morning was President's Day. The sheriff and our bishop knocked on my front door to tell me Becca was gone. As I began calling my brothers and sisters and we gathered the family together, we realized we needed to find our parents in Hawaii.

It was their first vacation in a very long time and they had not told us where they would be staying. We only knew the island they were staying on. Knowing we had to find them and tell them the news, we gathered as brothers and sisters, on our knees, asking our Heavenly Father to help us find our mom and dad.

After the prayer, we called hotels in Waikiki, one-by-one. The fourth one we called, they patched us through to our parents' room. Do you know how many hotels are on that island, as well as in the Waikiki area? It was a God moment and we knew it. God wanted them to know. He guided us in finding them.

My parents were not able to get a flight out until the next day, which was a long time to wait to get home and be with us. The next day as we picked up my parents from the airport, I held my mom and saw a very familiar, sad and heartbroken look on her face.

I said, "Mom, what are you thinking?"

And she said, "I am remember that Christmas of losing Ariann many years ago, as I was tucking you in bed and I asked you what I could get for you, and you said, 'I just want my baby back'." She then said, "I just want my baby back."

We hugged each other and we cried.

She then turned to me and said, "How do I do this?"

I said, "I don't know but I know you will do it."

That was quite the turn, wasn't it? My mom looking to me for answers on how to survive the loss of her child.

Don't get me wrong, I was so there for my mom in that time for her. I could easily be her mentor through it. I just did not *ever* want to come from, "I know exactly how you are feeling and how you are going to get through this." I did not. I could not truthfully tell my mom how to do the walk that was hers to take—not mine. I had taken mine already. It was her time to walk the grief walk. As sad and hard as that was for me.

The miracle of that moment, was that tender mercy God gave me around the death of Ariann, feeling complete healing with the death of my baby so I could say to my mom, "I have no idea how you are feeling or how you are going to do this."

My heartache was no longer resonating with her fresh heartache and pain. It was resonating as my heartache for me. Her heartache was separate and individual for her. It was not collapsed into one huge mess of heartache and pain, which can easily happen.

I was able to look at my mom and not say, "I do not know how you feel, yet I have been where you are." I had of course been where she was in a different time and place, and I might have known some of what she was going through but I didn't really. I knew my experience, but I didn't know how to walk in her shoes (much larger than mine).

I was not able to walk in her steps in that moment or any moment after. I can't profess to know her heartache or her pain or her loss. It was hers. As I said, I was always there for her. I could relate to her, felt some of her same heart break. But never could I say, "I *know* what you are going through."

To turn and have empathy towards that situation and to be able to say to her (and others), "You can do this. I know you will do it much better than I did." I believe she and my dad so did.

That was the gift of the Grace of God. He knew it, too.

I am hoping this make sense. I am hoping we can see it as their pain and heartache—not letting it collapse with our own pain. Ever.

I feel like looking at others 'doing the grief' thing and being able to say, "Oh wow, I don't know how you can be feeling, yet I believe in you and your ability to walk through this. I want to walk it with you," is a powerful show of empathy.

The only one who can truly know how they are feeling is the Savior. He is the one who comforts us endlessly through grief.

You may recall how the Savior instructed His apostles,

And I will pray the Father, and he shall give you another Comforter that he may abide with you forever; Even the Spirit of truth; whom the world cannot receive, because it seeth him not, neither knoweth him: but ye know him; for he dwelleth with you, and shall be in you. I will not leave you comfortless, I will come to you.

He will not leave us comfortless. He will come. He said He will and He will.

The week of Rebecca's funeral, I felt this promise He gave. I was grounded in my Savior and in my Heavenly Father. I felt the spirit of Rebecca and some really sweet experiences with feeling Ariann there with us, too. Of course those two found each other.

Becca holding Ariann

The day we went to the mortuary to dress Rebecca and to do her make-up, my aunt and I were at the end of the mortuary hall, talking about how we all chose this in a pre-life—a life before this one, which I believe we all experienced. I believe the life before this prepared us to do hard things. We knew we could do it, then.

My dad consistently kept saying, "You chose this."

My aunt and I were having a beautiful, tender conversation in the mortuary talking about how in the life before, we stood in that circle—my mom, my sister, me, and my daughter, saying how we would do it for the test and salvation of each other. As we stood there in the circle, we all agreed we would make it through this life honoring God's will.

It was not a conversation I could have had in the past, many years ago.

My mom was in the other room, dressing sweet Becca's body. She was down the hall from where my aunt and I were talking. There was a motion light in that hall which kept kicking on, but no one walked in the room. After this happened quite a few times, we finally knew. We were not alone.

The spirits of those two beautiful souls, Ariann and Rebecca, bounced back and forth from the room down the hall into our room. As they would come back they hit that motion light on again and again. It was all the goose-bump feelings. Tender mercies.

It is a beautiful tender moment to feel the hand of the Lord and those we love so very close at such a difficult time. Even though she was not physically there, we felt Rebecca powerfully pour into us that week spiritually—with Ariann, our Pampa, our Grandma Cottam, and other Angel family members right there with her, loving on us at that hard time.

During the time my mom dressed Rebecca, my dad was at the family restaurant, mopping the conference room floor. He shared with us later how he felt a hand on his shoulder and felt his mom reassuring him all was well.

"The Lord gives and the Lord taketh away, Blessed be the name of the Lord," she said to him.

God grants us these tender moments. A special and solemn spirit during the most difficult of times. The spirit of those who leave us and the spirits of those who have been gone. Our guardian angels, guiding us, even in harsh and yet tender moments. God is right there, orchestrating it all.

Isaiah 41:10 says,
Fear thou not; for I am with thee: be not dismayed; for I am thy God: I will strengthen thee; yea, I will help thee; yea, I will uphold thee with the right hand of my righteousness.

It is our foundation we must build upon. Firm foundation is in Jesus Christ and our God, no matter what.

It is in the strength of the Lord, I can do all things. And so can you.

You'll Never Walk Alone, sung by Josh Groban is an incredible song to listen to, to motivate us forward and on in our life.

Angels are sent to assist us along the way—Heavenly Angels and Earthly Angels. I think if we knew who walked with us every day, we would never feel alone again. We are not alone. We see them show up in ways of tender mercies daily.

David E. Bednar spoke about tender mercies saying,

> *We should not underestimate or overlook the power of the Lord's tender mercies. The simpleness, the sweetness, and the constancy of the tender mercies of the Lord will do much to fortify and protect us in the troubled times in which we do now and will yet live.*
>
> *When words cannot provide the solace we need or express the joy we feel, when it is simply futile to attempt to explain that which is unexplainable, when logic and reason cannot yield adequate understanding about the injustices and inequities of life, when mortal experience and evaluation are insufficient to produce a desired outcome, and when it seems that perhaps we are so totally alone, truly we are blessed by the tender mercies of the Lord and made mighty even unto the power of deliverance.*

I testify this to be so by sharing one more sweet story of a tender mercy after Rebecca's death. The Sunday after her funeral, my mom and I sat in our Church, with heavy, broken hearts. The Sacrament song began to play and the congregation sang, *As Now We Take The Sacrament*.

> *As now we take the Sacrament, Our thoughts are turned to thee. Thou Son of God, who lived for us, then died on Calvary.*
>
> *We contemplate thy lasting grace, thy boundless charity. To us the gift of life was given. For all eternity.*

As we sang the first verse of the song, our hearts were touched by the Savior who lived and then died for us on Calvary. His Grace is Lasting, His Charity boundless. It was because of the Son of God who lived for us all and then died for us all that the promise of life into eternity is so. That Becca lived. We knew it was truth being spoken to us at that moment in our heartache.

The second verse was another sweet reminder to us,

> *"As now our minds review the past, we know we must repent. The way to thee was righteousness, the way thy life was spent. Forgiveness is a gift from thee, we seek with pure intent. With Hands now pledged to do thy work, we take the Sacrament."*

We felt the Spirit flow through us as we sang that part. What a true gift to be able to partake of the Sacrament and be clean all over again, to be forgiven and to forgive, week after week. Especially that week in our grief. With hands clinging together, we both knew we still had work to do.

By the time we got to the third verse, tears streamed down our faces.

> *"As now we praise thy name in song, the blessings of this day, Will linger in our thankful hearts, and silently we pray. For courage to accept thy will, to listen and obey. We love thee Lord; our hearts our full, we'll walk thy chosen way."*

My mom and I sat with hands knitted tightly together, bawling our eyes out. We had such thankful hearts and we were very grateful to be so very blessed and to hear the words "for courage to accept His will" for that great loss in our life.

We do love our Lord and we will walk His way always.

It was a tender moment we'll never forget. Interestingly, it happens again and again for us when we hear that song, even on days I'm speaking or having a bad Sunday moment, like our first Corona virus Sunday—we sang it.

The song is a constant reminder that in His will, I can do all things, including accept and mourn the ones who die. Accept things as they are. Accepting His way is the only way. True happiness only comes from stepping in to Him, His will, His way, and His heart.

Tender mercies are real and I believe come to us from God, in His right time, in His the right way, and in Him bringing us to hope and light. Tender mercies are personal and individual ways God gives to us for strength, hope, assurance, and revelation. Through His gifts, we are able to walk forward after losing such important loved ones in our lives.

A few years after Becca died, I was home sleeping in my same bed she and I had had that sweet and final moment together before she died. I dreamed I was in an office working and the phone rang. I answered it, and the voice said, "Please hold for Rebecca Cottam."

Even in my dream I was so excited. I knew I wanted to talk to her. She quickly came on and asked me how I was and what was new. Then, she shared some very personal advice that I had been praying about and what I should do continuing down *my* path. The advice she gave me was an important piece of my life that had a huge impact on me. It was an amazing tender moment how prayers can be answered so personally by God, who knows all things ahead. That dream is as real today as it was eleven years or more ago.

Those happenings are not random or coincidences. They are God's hands reaching out to remind us He and the ones we love and mourn are with us always. Watch for the tender mercies. Hope for the tender mercies. Praise God for the tender mercies. Hold on tightly to them.

Share them when you are inspired to share them. Hold them sacred if you feel you need to. Know that it is through and given by God.

We had an interesting moment the week or so after the funeral of Rebecca. We had a family wedding down south of where we lived. Because of our recent loss, we felt it was important to attend as a whole family. It was difficult as we owned that family restaurant and the whole family leaving for a weekend was not easy, yet we made it happen. With losing someone so close to you, you realize what the most important part of this life is. As much as we love our family restaurant and the food, most important was the family—each other, to us.

It was a beautiful weekend for a wedding. We enjoyed the whole big extended family we have. The Holy Spirit was with us so powerfully during that time, especially from the funeral services and honoring her. Always a tender mercy to have the Spirit with you during hard times.

After the wedding party on Friday night, we chose to take a drive to Mesquite, Nevada as we were only forty-five minutes away. Mesquite is a little mini Vegas. We thought we would go down, grab some food, listen to some music, and drop a few coins. It was my brother Ben, his wife, Joni, Becca's boyfriend, Corey, and me. As we drove, we listened to Becca's favorite songs and shared more sweet memories of her.

As we pulled into the parking lot of the casino, the sweet Holy Spirit and Rebecca's sweet spirit were so close and very powerful in comforting and reminding us of what was important.

We walked through the casino's large automatic doors and immediately felt a rush of complete emptiness. The four of us stood by the front doors, wondering what had just happened? We felt completely void of the Holy Spirit and we knew we stood alone in the casino.

Rebecca was no longer with us. The Holy Spirit had also taken its departure. We stood there feeling very alone. We lasted less than thirty minutes, as we *knew* it was not where we wanted to be. It was a difficult moment without the presence of the Holy Spirit, and the one we loved not able to be with us because of the worldly place we had ventured into.

I doubt I'll ever forget that moment and the complete loneliness I felt. I want to be in a place that inspires, that allows the Holy Spirit and my angels who have gone to reside with me. It puts a whole new meaning to the beautiful scripture that says, "Wherefore, stand ye in holy places, and be not moved, until the day of the Lord come; for behold, it cometh quickly, saith the Lord." (D&C 87:8)

The song I leave you touches me with these truths every time I hear it—a song my friend, Dan Truman and *Diamond Rio* sings.

There are more than angels watching over all of us, I believe.

I Believe, *by Diamond Rio.*

I believe, in the tender mercies and the God moments. Do you? I believe His will is the only way. Do you?

Journaling Thoughts

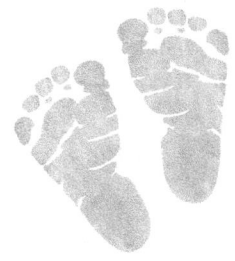

* 22 *

THE ATONEMENT of JESUS CHRIST

"He is there! Our prayers are heard. And when we weep, He and the Angels of Heaven weep with us." ~Jeffrey R Holland

HE IS THERE. HE HEARS our cries. He knows our hearts. He is weeping with us, as our angels are, too… this is such a humbling quote that touches my soul.

Christ said, "Blessed are those who mourn, for they shall be comforted." Many of the Beatitudes are said with an eternal perspective in mind.

The pure in heart may not see God today. The meek don't currently inherit the earth. The poor in spirit don't have the kingdom of heaven right now.

The hungry and thirsty are just that right now—*hungry and thirsty*. The promises of the verses Christ shares may have some delay or not even be experienced in this life. And so, it makes sense if the act of being comforted takes time in our life, as well.

Although we'll feel the joy, peace, strength, and comfort that comes through the Atonement of Jesus Christ, there still may be seasons when you feel deep sorrows, again and again. Heartache may not have a clear end, in this life.

Through Christ's atonement and resurrection, there is undoubtedly an end.

If you are in the mourning time of your life, give yourself grace. Christ does. Give yourself time. Christ will. Give yourself understanding. Christ totally understands. There is a fullness of joy ahead. I now know this to be truth.

I did not have a solid testimony of the Atonement of Jesus Christ when Ariann died. I was raised being taught about Him and His Atonement but I didn't get it at the time of her death. For so many years, my heart was just broken and hurt from the loss of my sweet baby. I did not feel Him weeping with me, or God hearing me. I didn't want to. Remember, I was also so far pushed away from God, I didn't let myself feel Him. I knew there was a Father in Heaven but knowing He knew me and was there for me was another thought.

What I did not know was the power of deliverance from my trials was in place and ready for me to step unto it, no matter.

It is called the Atonement of Jesus Christ. I did not turn unto it at the time of Ari's death. It didn't matter. He still bore it. All of it. He stood ready for me to turn unto Him when I was ready.

Although painful, grief can bring us closer to the Savior, if we choose to let it. The beautiful gift of this life is the Atonement of Jesus Christ.

The Savior's Atonement and Resurrection gave Him the power to strengthen us in our trials and even deliver us from them:

> *And behold, he shall be born of Mary, at Jerusalem which is the land of our forefathers, she being a virgin, a precious and chosen vessel, who shall be overshadowed*

and conceive by the power of the Holy Ghost, and bring forth a son, yea, even the Son of God.

And he shall go forth, suffering pains and afflictions and temptations of every kind; and this that the word might be fulfilled which saith he will take upon him the pains and the sicknesses of his people.

And he will take upon him death, that he may lose the bands of death which bind his people; and he will take upon him their infirmities, that his bowels may be filled with mercy, according to the flesh, that he may know according to the flesh how to succor his people according to their infirmities. (Alma 7:10–12)

I love this amazing scripture coming from Alma who came to know this truth, 'That He may *know* according to the flesh *how* to succor His people.' He knows. He felt it. It's the access through which we have to peace, strength and healing.

The very best way to heal your wounded heart is by tapping into that enabling power of the Atonement of Jesus Christ. My many tender mercies, I believe, came because I finally turned unto Him, believed in Him, and sought after Him.

So, when you are encompassed by sorrows and grief, behold the Man. When you feel lost or forgotten, behold the Man.

When you are despairing, deserted, doubting, damaged, or defeated, behold the Man. He will comfort you.

He will heal you and give meaning to your journey. He will pour out His Spirit and fill your heart with exceeding joy.

He gives 'power to the faint; and to them that have no might he increaseth strength'. ~ Dieter F. Uchtdorf

He gives a time to mourn and the time to find peace through His Atonement.

Elder Scott proclaimed in his last general conference talk in October, 2014:

We came to mortal life precisely to grow from trials and testing. Challenges help us become more like our Father in Heaven, and the Atonement of Jesus Christ makes it possible to endure those challenges. I testify that as we actively come unto Him, we can endure every temptation, every heartache, every challenge we face.

For those of us who have lost loved ones, that road you look ahead is filled with many emotions, including lonely and immense sadness. It seems even more so difficult for those without a knowledge and testimony of the Atonement and Resurrection of the Savior Jesus Christ.

A few weeks after my sister Rebecca's death, I walked into our family restaurant to see and hear my parents comforting her boyfriend's parents. They did not have the Gospel of Jesus Christ in their lives. My parents testified and encouraged his parents to look up, find hope and trust in God.

Luke described an exact scene in the Bible. In Luke 24:19–21, you may recall Christ's two doubtful disciples on the road to Emmaus. I am sure they were talking about His precious death and how final it all was to them, as that was all that they knew; Death being final. The resurrected Lord drew near to them and asked, "Why are you sad?"

Luke gave us the answer,

And they said unto him, Concerning Jesus of Nazareth, which was a prophet mighty in deed and word before God and all the people. And how the chief priests and our rulers delivered him to be condemned to death, and have crucified him. But we trusted that it had been he which should have redeemed Israel.

We need to trust and believe He did redeem for us. For so many reasons for us, He bore and felt it all. Ironically, for me there would be *No* Christmas morning without *that* Easter morning when He arose from His death. His death has given us life. Eternal life. Forever. That we may *all* live forever. There could be no redemption for any of mankind save it were through the sufferings of Christ, and the Atonement of His blood for us.

Thomas S. Monson said, "There are times when we will experience heartbreaking sorrow, when we will grieve and when we may be tested to our limits."

"However," he continued, "such difficulties allow us to change for the better, to rebuild our lives in the way our Heavenly Father teaches us, and to become something from what we were—better than what we were, more understanding than what we were, more emphatic than what we were, with stronger testimonies than we had before."

To change for the better, to rebuild our lives as our Father would have us following His example, and to become better, more understanding, more emphatic and solid in testimonies, is the ultimate achievement. That is the gift of trials and death in our lives.

Death is just a part of our existence here on the earth. The hardest part. Nevertheless, through the Atonement and Resurrection of His Son, Heavenly Father has provided a way for us not only to overcome death but also to be comforted and healed after the loss of loved ones.

It is through the power of the Atonement, that "the sting of death" can be replaced by the "peace that the Spirit brings." (Alma 22:14)

Merrill J. Bateman said,

> *Just as the lame man at the Pool of Bethesda needed someone stronger than himself to be healed, so we are dependent on the miracles of Christ's Atonement if our souls are to be made whole from grief, sorrow, and sin. Death's sting is softened as Jesus bears the believers' grief and comforts them through the Holy Spirit. Through Christ, broken hearts are mended and peace replaces anxiety and sorrow.*

As I look back on me stepping into that grace of the Atonement, I felt unworthy of it. I also felt Him say, "I did it for you as much as anyone else."

It had been a long, dark journey for me without that light of His enabling power in my life.

Some nights were much longer and darker than others and seemed to go on forever, but the morning always follows. Death brings deep sorrow, but our joy will exceed our ability to comprehend when our reunion with deceased loved ones finally comes. Peace is not reserved for the next life only—we can feel peace now, even in the very moment we are feeling pain. How thankful we can be for the sacrifice of our Savior and the healing power His Atonement can bring us in spite of our grief. When we find that joy, oh, what a gift it is. It was for me.

"Weeping may endure for a night, but joy cometh in the morning." (Psalm 30:5)

We can draw comfort and peace in our healing from our knowledge and testimony that it was He who redeemed us.

It was He who "[broke] the bands of death." (Mosiah 15:23)

It was He who became "the first fruits of them that slept." (1 Corinthians 15:20)

It was He who made possible, by the power of the priesthood, the temple covenants that bind us forever to those we "have loved long since, and lost awhile." It is through the beautiful gift of the Atonement we can access the Savior's power of deliverance. It is what strengthens me. I pray it can strengthen you.

The Savior has said, "Thou shalt live together in love, insomuch that thou shalt weep for the loss of them that die." (D&C 42:45)

I have learned grief is the price we pay for living together and loving with our whole hearts.

Each of us will be tested by facing the death of someone we love and adore. If you do not know that heartbreak yet, you will most likely experience it. For me, the most difficult part of the test of physical loss of someone close to me, was what do we do with the sadness, the loneliness, the broken heart? The grief can go on and on, like a chronic life ache.

I know there is no comparison of the two deaths I personally experienced, between my own baby and my baby sister. Yet it seemed for me when I accepted and stepped into being a true child of God years after my baby died, I found so much peace, comfort, and healing. The death of my sister was sad, heartbreaking, and difficult, yet it felt lighter, easier, hopeful in peace. I know it seems like I can't compare those but for me, I knew, Knowing my Savior and my God so powerfully at that time, it was so much easier to find the *joy*.

> *I feel to exhort you with heartfelt expression. Be of good cheer—be not disheartened; for assuredly the day rapidly comes when your tears shall be dried, your hearts comforted. ~ Lorenzo Snow*

The hope I have, I know, comes through the Savior's Atonement and Resurrection. It gave Him the power to deliver us in such trials.

Through His Atoning experience, He personally came to know our griefs. He could have come to know and learn of them by the inspiration of the Spirit, but He chose instead to know by actually experiencing them for Himself. I do not know when and how He did, but I know He did.

Henry B. Eyring said,

> *Good people around you will try to understand your grief at the passing of a loved one. They may feel grief themselves. The Savior not only understands and feels grief but also feels your personal grief that only you feel. And He knows you perfectly. He knows your heart.*

We trusted it had been He who should have redeemed Israel. It works in the same way as the deliverance from the trial that comes in facing the death of a loved one. Just as that deliverance is not always to have the life of a loved one spared, the deliverance from other trials may not be to remove them.

The Lord may not give relief until we develop faith to make choices that will bring the power of the Atonement to work in our lives. He does not require that out of indifference but out of love for us. Only the Savior understands and feels grief, but He also feels *your* personal grief only you feel.

He perfectly knows you. He knows your heart. He knows all because He felt it all.

A friend wrote to me after her son's death,

> *A nearly five-year battle with emotional 'darkness and gloom' in varying degrees takes you to the very edge of your capacities, resolve, faith, and patience. After days of suffering, you are tired. After weeks of suffering, you are exhausted. After months of suffering, you begin to lose your ground. After years of suffering, you submit to the possibility that you'll never get better again. Hope becomes the most precious, and elusive, of gifts. In short, I'm not sure I know how I got through*

> *this trial, save it was the Savior and His Atonement. It's the only explanation. I can't explain how I know this, except that I do. Because of Him, I got through this.*

I could not have said it better. I cannot explain how I survived it, only by finally giving it up to Him to bear and carry it for me. His Atonement bears all things including grief and heartache, loss and despair, sadness and loneliness.

When tragedies overtake us, when life hurts so much we can't breathe, when we've taken a beating like the man on the road to Jericho and have been left for dead, Jesus comes along and pours oil into our wounds, tenderly lifts us up, takes us to an inn, looks after us.

To those of us in grief, He says, "I will ease the burdens which are put upon your shoulders, that even you cannot feel them upon your backs, that ye may know of a surety that I, the Lord God, do visit my people in their afflictions." (Mosiah 24:15)

Christ heals all.

> *God did not create our spirits to be independent of Him. Our Lord and Savior, Jesus Christ, through the incalculable gift of His Atonement, not only saves us from death and offers us, through repentance, forgiveness for our sins, but He also stands ready to save us from the sorrows and pains of our wounded souls. ~ Neil L. Anderson*

We will be resurrected, including our loved ones, because of the Atonement of Jesus Christ. The reunion we'll have with them will be glorious and beautiful, with bodies that are perfect—that will never die, nor age, nor become infirm.

When the Savior appeared to His Apostles after the Resurrection, He not only reassured them in their grief but also all of us who might ever grieve.

He reassured them and us this way, "Peace be unto you...Behold my hands and my feet, that it is I myself: handle me, and see; for a spirit hath not flesh and bones, as ye see me have." (Luke 24:36, 39)

Jesus Christ offers us the most amazing gift of Peace through His wounded hands and body.

Where Can I Turn For Peace, *words by Emma Lou Thayne, 1924–2014*

Journaling Thoughts

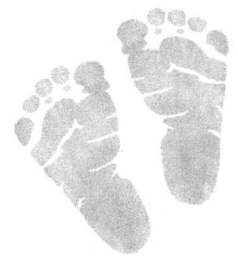

* 23 *

AN ETERNAL PERSPECTIVE
WHAT? WHY? HOW?

"Looking forward with an Eternal Perspective, gives one hope, *a reason to look up and feel gratitude for even the smallest of light." ~ Rosemary M Wixom*

At the funeral of my baby on December 27th, Grandma Matie Cottam came in, put an arm around me in the 'Cottam side hug' that they do, and said, "The Lord gave, and the Lord hath taketh away. Blessed be the name of the Lord."

I hesitantly admit, from the time my baby died, this 'Eternal Perspective' they spoke about, did not come easy or happen overnight. It took me many years. *A whole lot of years.* A lot of reading, studying, and pondering the concept of an Eternal Perspective.

What does that even mean? I know there is still so much to it that I have not grasped but I want to give a tiny, little bit to you about this subject. It's crucial in the healing process.

We could define eternal perspective as, "To look at life in light of the life to come, to accept eternity as the dominant reality."

For me, having an eternal perspective means evaluating the beliefs, events, decisions, and actions of life from God's point of view. It's using God's values as the measuring stick with which we evaluate life. It's recognizing that everything done in the present has an eternal consequence and should be evaluated in that light. Looking at life through spiritual eyes, as God does.

> *We came to this earth that we might have a body and present it pure before God in the celestial kingdom. The great principle of happiness consists in having a body.* ~ Joseph Smith

Coming to this earth and having a physical body is crucial to eternal life and the hereafter.

We were each divinely appointed to this life. We and all that we do are an important part of God's plan. His forever plan. We accepted His plan for our divine destiny.

Joseph Fielding Smith said,

> *At one time we were in the presence of our Eternal Father. There is not a soul in this room, not one, who has not seen him. You do not remember it, I do not remember it, but nevertheless there was a time before we ever came into this world when we dwelt in his presence. We knew what kind of a being he is.*
>
> *One thing we saw was how glorious he is. Another thing, how great was his wisdom, his understanding, how wonderful was his power and his inspiration. And we wanted to be like him. And because we wanted to be like him, we are here. We could not be like him and stay in his presence, because we did not have glorious bodies of flesh and bones. We were just spirits, and the spirit does not have flesh and bones.*
>
> *But we saw him in his glory and it was made known to us that by keeping his commandments and observing*

every covenant that would be given to us on this earth, we could come back again into his presence, receiving our bodies in the resurrection from the dead—our spirits and bodies being united again, inseparably, never again to be divided.

It is and was important for Ariann's eternal and divine destiny to come and obtain a body to have His Glory upon her. She only had to be here for four months for her Divine mission. I can chose to view the world through *spiritual* eyes, with God's perspective or I can simply view the world through *physical* eyes and fail to grasp the eternal of it. My spiritual view of life will greatly affect my attitude, thinking, and my actions.

Maybe my Grandma Cottam's scriptural reference might have had me think for a minute, when she said it. What she said has never left me for some reason. It didn't bring heartache in the moment, or maybe it did. A little *ouch* at the time. It was tough to hear. My tough-hearted Grandma's words brought more peace to me than they did hurt.

What she said was a scripture reference from Job 1:21 where he says, "Naked came I out of my mother's womb, and naked shall I return thither: the LORD gave, and the LORD hath taken away; blessed be the name of the LORD."

Okay...Most of us who went to Sunday school know what happened to Job in his test and trials of life. That 'poor' Job, he endured a *lot*!

It was a bit of a shock to me to think the Lord just takes like that. It's probably why I spent many years angry at the Lord for taking that precious soul from me. It was an interesting moment for me. I was raised Christian and so the Lord was a big part of our everyday lives, our prayers, our daily doings and our weekly worships. It came as quite a punch to be given to me at such a young age—that He takes away babies, just like that.

As you have probably noticed and as I have stated a few times in this book, I am a Christian. I am a member of the Church of Jesus Christ of Latter Day Saints. I love it! I truly love it, now. I am eternally grateful for goodly and Christ-like parents who from the time I was a very little girl taught me home-centered, gospel principles where I believe I gained a small glimpse at eternal perspective. Very tiny.

Even though I didn't have much of it when that sweet baby of mine died.

My parents taught me the *Plan of Happiness and Salvation* and I believed it. I loved it. The *Plan of Salvation* that was taught to me answered the simple questions so many of us ask, "Where did we come from? Why are we here? Where are we going?"

It explains it like this: God is the Father of our Spirits. We are literally His children, and He loves us. We lived as Spirit Children of our Father in Heaven before we were born on this earth. In a pre-earth life. We were not, however, like our Heavenly Father, nor could we ever become like Him and enjoy the blessings He enjoys without the experience of living in mortality with a physical body. On this Earth.

God's whole purpose—His work and His glory—is to enable each of us to enjoy His blessings. He has provided a perfect plan to accomplish His purpose. We understood and accepted His plan before we came to the earth.

I accepted only to have Ariann for four months on this earth. She accepted His plan, as well.

In the scriptures, God's plan is called a merciful plan, the plan of happiness, the plan of redemption, and the plan of salvation.

Jesus Christ was central to God's plan. Through His Atonement, Jesus Christ fulfilled His Father's purpose and made it possible for each of us to enjoy immortality and exaltation. Satan, or the devil, is an enemy to God's plan.

Agency, or the ability to choose, is one of God's greatest gifts to His children. Our eternal progression depends on how we use that gift. We must choose whether to follow Jesus Christ or to follow Satan. Although, we are physically separated from God during life on earth, He wants every one of His children to find peace in this life and a fullness of joy in His presence after this life. He wants us to become like Him. To be with Him again. We are His children and He wants us to come home to Him as we want our own babies to come home to us.

Through all of that, here is what I know: I know there is a God—He does exist, He knows and loves each one of us. You and me, as His own children. As we are. God gave us free agency. He allows suffering for our own growth. Suffering allows us to grow closer to Him. To have patience, faith, and compassion for others. Turning to God in faith gives us the truths to answer even the hardest questions we have. If we turn to Him and not away from Him, like I did for so long.

Seeing life from an eternal perspective is also *knowing* God provides angels to be with us always. Even after Adam and Eve left the Garden of Eden, an angel appeared unto them teaching them the meaning of sacrifice and the atoning role of the promised Savior who was to come and redeem them. Mary, the mother of Jesus, was sent an angel to testify to her that she would carry a son, and call his name Jesus, and He would save the world. Elizabeth was sent the same angel to tell her she was with child, as was Mary, her cousin.

From the beginning down through the dispensations, God used angels as His emissaries in conveying love and concern for His children. But most often, to comfort, to provide some form of merciful attention, and guidance in difficult times.

In times of special need, He sent angels, divine messengers, to bless His children, reassure them heaven was always very close and His help was always very near.

"If you knew who walked with you."

Angels have not stopped ministering and guiding us, even in this day.

I love the scripture in Matthew 10:29 which says, "Not a single sparrow can fall to the ground without your Father knowing it."

He knows all. He has the eternal perspective of all—the loss we feel, the grief we suffer and will deal with, the happiness we will find, and the way we are to go in our journey.

As I look back, I stood that way during the loss of Becca. I saw myself step in to Him, trusting and praying to Him. I found my testimony strengthen during that hard time. I saw myself sad and felt the emotional grief ride, yet I was grounded in Jesus Christ. Solid in knowing He had me. He knew my heartache. He knew my mom's pain and heartache around her loss. He was there through it all.

Having an eternal perspective begins with knowing God is an all-loving Father in Heaven and not a punishing God. He loves us and just like with our children, we want them to be happy and have a great life, so does He. But life happens, choices are made, challenges are our opportunities to grow. He allows certain trials to come upon us.

One of the most difficult things said to me, and yet the one comment that stuck solid with me at the time of my baby's death, was when my dad said to me, "Remember that you chose this."

What?! Why would I choose this for myself? Why would I put myself through this? Why me? Why am I dealing with this loss? This trial, this heartache? Why? Why me? Why Christmas Day? (That one still seems like a valid question to me.)

My dad said, "This is the lesson you asked for, the one you are going to have to endure for life. The one you've asked for as you said you wanted to learn these things. You said you wanted to do God's will and you said you would be a part of doing this for Ariann and for Him."

What he basically said was "God said, 'here are some experiences you can have in this life to help you become the best you,' and it sounded good at the time and you said, 'I'll take it.'"

Like Job, who lost everything and was being tested, he knew it was part of his life plan. He never cursed God. Only praised Him. He seemed to grasp the eternal perspective and that he chose it.

He testified of the Savior saying, "For I know that my Redeemer liveth, and that He shall stand at the latter day upon the earth."

Being able to be like Job and to say, "This is part of my life's journey." There is such power in that.

Yet, when I was going through it at the time, I was like, "No way, I didn't chose this, Father. Really?" I was twenty-one and I thought I knew life. Yet, now looking back, it's like, "Yep, I did. I chose that."

I would choose it again. I would choose having her in my arms for the four months, giving her the perfect eternal life she needed and gaining all the promised blessings that are coming from such a trial if I can just endure. Eternal perspective shift, right there!

The question is—Would you choose it all over again?

I feel after we go through the hard, we say, "I would do that again, to learn what I've learned, to become who I've become from that trial." Like Joseph in Egypt—"But God."

I know losing Ariann has made me a different, empathetic, compassionate, and loving human being. Way different, better than whom I was before.

I once attended a funeral for a young missionary who was killed in an accident. The missionary's father spoke in the service and described the heartache of an unexpected mortal separation from a beloved child. He forthrightly declared he personally did not understand the reasons or timing for such an event. But, I always will remember that good man also declaring he knew God knew the reasons and timing for the passing of his child—and that was good enough for him.

He told the congregation he and his family, though sorrowful, would be fine—their testimonies remained firm and steadfast.

He concluded his remarks with a declaration: "I want you to know that as far as the gospel of Jesus Christ is concerned, our family is all in. We are all in."

Though the loss of a dear loved one was heart wrenching and difficult, the members of that valiant family were spiritually prepared to prove they could learn lessons of eternal importance through the events they suffered.

Understanding and seeing life from an eternal perspective changes everything as we see it, like we look through different glasses at it.

God wants us to see an eternal perspective instead of from the mortal perspective we view way too much. He wants us to see beyond today and look into the eternities.

Hanging on to eternity is letting go of the world and the human in us. Having an eternal perspective in this life is the key to living a true Christ-like life.

2 Corinthians 4:18 says, "So we fix our eyes not on what is seen, but is unseen, since what is seen is temporary, but what is unseen is eternal."

We are in an unseen life. Sometimes it's difficult to keep the eternal prospective in our sights because it's unseen for us. Yet, we keep moving forward as we thrive in life.

Spencer W. Kimball said,

> *We knew before we were born that we were coming to the earth for bodies and experience and that we would have joys and sorrows, pain and comforts, ease and hardships, health and sickness, successes and disappointments; and we knew also that we would die. We accepted all these eventualities with a glad heart eager to accept both the favorable and unfavorable. We were willing to come and take life as it came.*

We knew this and we said 'yes' to it for our own earthy experience.

My question is, "How do I gain an eternal perspective?"

To study and meditate on God's ways and His values—you cannot know God's will unless you know His Words, through scripture.

Daily scripture and prayer draw us closer to an eternal perspective. Choose daily to study, pray, and to ask for the eternal perspective on all you are dealing with. To accept difficulties and to progress through them. To make choices that are part of who we truly are. To *accept*. To center our lives around our divine potential—we are children of a Father in Heaven who loves us. Despite what we say or do.

President George Q. Cannon once taught:

> *No matter how serious the trial, how deep the distress, how great the affliction, [God] will never desert us. He never has, and He never will. He cannot do it. It is not His character [to do so]. ... He will [always] stand by us.*

> *We may pass through the fiery furnace; we may pass through deep waters; but we shall not be consumed nor overwhelmed. We shall emerge from all these trials and difficulties the better and purer for them.*

My trials have been serious, my distress deep, and my affliction great. God has not deserted me, nor will he ever. He loves me and bears me up as I walk my valleys. I can face them because of Him guiding my life.

> *Living the gospel does not mean the storms of life will pass us by, but we will be better prepared to face them with serenity and peace. 'Search diligently, pray always, and be believing,' the Lord admonished, 'and all things shall work together for your good, if ye walk uprightly.' ~ Joseph B. Wirthlin*

Every minute someone leaves this world behind. We are all in "the line" without knowing it. We never know how many people are before us. We cannot move to the back of the line. We cannot step out of the line. We cannot avoid the line.

So, while we wait in line:
- Make moments count.
- Make priorities.
- Make the time.
- Make your gifts known.
- Make a nobody feel like a somebody.
- Make Kindness your life theme.
- Make your voice heard.
- Make the small things big.
- Make someone smile.
- Make the change.

- Make love.
- Make up.
- Make peace.
- Make sure to tell your people they are loved.
- Make sure to have no regrets.
- Make sure you are ready.

The end of the line quickly comes for us all.

A sweet song that was shared in a powerful church service I attended one time, was sung by a 'special needs' group. The words are perfect in the answering of the *why* questions?

The Test *by Janice Kapp Perry.*

We recently realized that as we buried Dirk's mom. Even at eighty-four, battling with cancer, we did not have enough time, and we were not ready to say goodbye.

Yet, it's not the end. She is with us and we will see her again.

Dieder F. Uchtdorf said, "We are eternal beings, endings are not in our destiny."

The Sweetest Gift *by the Piano Guys and Chris Aven*

The sweetest gift is knowing where you are, Ariann. You are in His arms, the Son of God. I know this to be true.

Journaling Thoughts

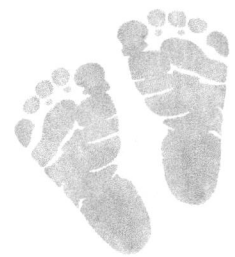

* 24 *

MOVING BEYOND and THRIVING FORWARD

"Even if you cannot always see that silver lining on your clouds, God can, for He is the very source of the light you seek." ~ Jeffrey R. Holland,

SOMETHING WILL ALWAYS BE MISSING, a piece of ourselves will always not be there. As we move forward, look at ways we can protect ourselves and make our life great.

Here is a list to pick from. Slowly start on one or two:

- Let go of things we can't control.
- Avoid comparing ourselves to others.
- Keep our faith larger than our fears.
- Don't do things that don't feel right to us.
- Spend time alone.
- Know it's okay to do it our way for now, for a while.
- Avoid gossiping or bashing others.

- Be patient with ourselves.
- Speak kindly to ourselves and others.
- Please us right now, not others.
- Create healthy boundaries.
- Say no if we need to.
- Stay away from people who drain our energy.
- Ignore opinions that don't uplift us. Unfriend, block, walk away, find support elsewhere.
- Ask for help when we do need it.
- *Know when we are in trouble*—Please make sure you get help when you need it!

> *Once the storm is over you won't remember how you made it through, how you managed to survive. You won't even be sure, in fact whether the storm is over. But one thing is certain, when you come out of the storm you will not even be the same person who walked in. That is what the storm is all about.* ~ Haruki Murakami

Wherever we are in the journey, remember we need to take small steps toward the things that make our lives better and make us happy. We accept the changed self that we are. We cannot go back to where we were, yet we can go forward to where we choose to be.

We need to acknowledge what is healthy around us and maybe step back from what is not healthy surrounding us.

Moving forward is all part of life. God will open windows and then doors for you. Just step forward. Miracles will happen. Healing will take place. Don't quit. Keep moving forward. Your greatest days are ahead of you.

> *"Go back?" he thought. "No good at all! Go sideways? Impossible! Go forward? Only thing to do!*

On we go!" So up he got, and trotted along with his little sword held in front of him and one hand feeling the wall, and his heart all of a patter and a pitter." ~ J.R.R. Tolkien, The Hobbit

One of the blessings I found in my grief is to be able to love and care for myself during that time. At times, when it feels like your world has fallen apart, it's most important to focus on *you* and healing *you*. That's difficult for some of us, especially if we have kids or families or jobs and other distractions we have to take care of. Focusing on some self-care healing can really help your mind and body recover from loss and trials.

Self-care time can mean so much and can be as inexpensive as you want it to be. It can mean just starting to do one thing today that you didn't do yesterday. Start by taking a shower and washing your hair. Start by putting on some make up. Start by doing your hair pretty. Start by getting dressed and out of your lounge clothes. Start by drinking a refreshing cup of water. Start by reading one page in a self-improvement book. Start by taking one walk. Start by going out one time this week. Start by writing one paragraph. Start today by doing one thing.

Then repeat that tomorrow.

What Is self-care? Self-care is being willing and committed to rejuvenate your soul and finding your center—the place of unshakable peace and stability where you can weather the storms of life. Being intentional in our self-care practice is the greatest act of love we can give ourselves.

Lucille Ball said, "Love yourself first, and everything else falls in line. You really have to love yourself to get anything done in this world."

I watched a close friend go through a very difficult trial in her life. The one thing she found to really make a difference for her peace of mind and for her to weather the storm she was going through, was daily self-care. For her it was yoga and meditation daily.

Self care looks totally different for each of us. Self care can take many forms, yet it is necessary to find grounding and balancing for you right now. Another friend found her juju in hiking every day in nature. For me it is sun, water, and gardening. I love a swimming pool, an ocean (if I am lucky), or even my hot baths with bath salts and essential oils. *Ahhhhhhhhh.*

The One-Minute, Four-Step Self-Care Practice
By Rev. Elizabeth Longo

> *It is crucial to our well-being that self-care be part of our daily routine, especially during our busiest times. It does not have to take much time or money. Here is a practice that can be done many times during the day: Pause. Take a moment to disconnect from the world of time and space and simply be. Notice. Pay attention to your thoughts, feelings, and body sensations. Relax. Accept the moment as it is.*
>
> *Breathe. Take a couple of deep breaths. This will take the attention away from worry thoughts as you allow yourself to relax into your natural state, centered and aligned with your Spirit. Be Grateful. Bring your attention to your heart. You might want to place your hand on your heart, feel the heartbeat, and thank yourself for taking a minute to care for your soul. Then find one thing you are grateful for in that moment.*

I hope you can learn to practice some self-love and caring for yourself. Take some time for you. I feel like one of the hardest parts of going through the grief is to really take care of yourself and be able to speak what you need and when you need it.

There are four types of self care: Physical, Emotional, Social, and Spiritual.

Physical self care shows up as sleep, naps/rest, baths, healthy food, stretching, yoga, walking, hiking—any physical activity or release.

Emotional self care looks like managing stress, emotional maturity, forgiveness, compassion, kindness, meditation, going within and working on self.

Social self care could be setting boundaries, support systems and groups, positive social interaction, communication, therapy, friends lunch or shopping, time with people, asking for support.

Spiritual self care is time alone, meditation, prayer, yoga, connection with God, attending temple or church, journaling, nature walks or hike, a sacred space to be.

Here is a list to get you going:

- Watch a funny movie.
- Music-music-music—so self-caring. Find soul-searching or loud-blasting music and play it.
- Friends lunch.
- Pedicures.
- Massage.
- Go to a temple or church.
- Sit still and pray.
- Go to a mountain and sit in nature—meditate and pray.
- Make something crafty—I love making wall and door wreaths.
- Simplify your life.
- Gratitude Journal—find five things daily you are grateful for.
- Spend time with people who uplift your soul.

- Do something different for you.
- Unplug your phone, take a rest from all technology at least for an hour a day.
- Instead of your phone, plug in to Spirit—pray, meditate, and write.
- Listen to the still, small voice within.
- Move your body more.
- Stretch or do yoga.
- Watch comedy—give yourself permission to laugh.
- Go for a hike.
- Eat more fruit and veggies—they make you happy.
- Try to eliminate sugar—it brings low energy.
- For me, *no chips*. No carbs.
- Practice Yoga.
- Meditate.
- Plan a get-away.
- Take a trip.
- Eat yummy/comfort food (ironically that's chips and mashed potatoes for me).
- Give yourself permission to sit, cry, and mourn—schedule it in.
- *Epson* bath salts with essential oils and a hot soaking bath, foot bath, or shower.
- Find a quiet spot and be.
- Read a book.
- Arise early and have some scheduled time with God.
- Pray.
- Write in your journal—record the good, the bad, and the ugly. Give yourself permission to write it down.

- Sappy movie day or night. Invite a friend or do it with just you.
- Take a long nap. No guilt.
- Give a hug.
- Ask for a hug or loves.
- Ask for attention from someone you need it from.
- Give yourself permission to feel good.
- Walk in nature or around the block.
- Talk to a professional or someone—Share it all.
- Exercise, even for just five minutes.
- Find someone to serve or love on.
- Say 'no' to things that don't support you.
- Go to bed early.
- Say 'yes' to doing something.
- Facial.
- Pamper you with a spa day.
- Shopping.
- CHOCOLATE-CHOCOLATE-CHOCOLATE!
- Slug it—do nothing at all and be okay with it.
- Listen more to your heart.
- Do what you want to do.

It sounds so simple, but little things like getting enough sleep and eating as healthy as possible can make a huge difference on how we feel emotionally. Lack of sleep can cause problems with depression and anxiety. Also, exercising has been proven to significantly reduce symptoms of depression. So, if you're feeling down, stuck, or overwhelmed, take a walk or head to the gym for a little while.

Even at your lowest moments, please take the time and energy to eat well, exercise, and sleep. You might need to get some sleep aids for a time but consider essential oils, too. (See recommendations in next chapter.)

A while back ago, I was on a road trip for work by myself. I had my playlist running as I was driving down the road. A song came on that was so very beautiful for me in that moment. I want to share the lyrics with you so please scan it, download, and listen:

I'll Be Okay *by Lydia Laird*

We are all okay when we stop, breathe, and remember who we are and who has us always.

Journaling Thoughts

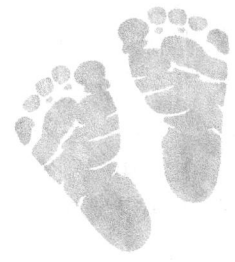

* 25 *

Healing—from the Good of the Earth

And by the river upon the bank thereof, on this side and on that side, shall grow all trees for meat, whose leaf shall not fade; and the fruit thereof shall be for meat, and the leaf thereof for medicine. ~ Ezekial 47:12

And the leaves of the tree are for the healing of the nations. ~ Revelations 2:22

Twenty years ago I was introduced to essential oils. I had a powerful story with being able to stop my daughter's nosebleeds by using essential oils. I began using them in bath salts for relaxing, aromatherapy baths, for headaches, and for helping me sleep and shut my brain down. I also love to use them for cleaning and laundry.

Over ten years ago, I was introduced to a company that was so different than any essential oils I had ever used. A medicinal grade of essential oils.

Pure.

Potent.

Powerful.

A CPTG (Certified Pure Tested Grade) brand of essential oils.

One of my first *ah-ha* experiences with that company and their oils was sitting at a class being educated on the gift of essential oils for pain, digestive issues, immune support, and moods.

Right after Ariann died, I started to deal with anxiety attacks, which *they* told me were normal even though they didn't feel normal. I dealt with the anxiety attacks for almost twenty years.

As one specific oil came around and I inhaled it, my body literally leaned forward over the bottle. I felt like I needed to jump into the bottle. In learning about the emotional benefit of that oil, I learned it was an oil specifically targeted for anxious feelings and feeling panicky. This oil called *The Grounding Blend* is made from a myriad of tree oils.

If you look at a tree, it's pretty grounded, rooted, stable and solid:

The Grounding Blend

It became my favorite essential oil. Still is today.

After I was introduced to that company, and their oils, I implemented them into my everyday life. I quickly quit having crazy anxiety. It made sense, as the essential oils created a grounding effect, an in-the-moment, this-is-my-life, happy-to-be-in-it state of being. I found myself healthier, smiling more, happier, and more present with my life as it was, and the people around me.

The essential oils and vitamins were a game changer for me and my moods, my losing-Ariann depression, and anxiety. I was not down sick as often as I use to be, I lost weight, and I felt the brain fog and confusion lift. It was glorious. I loved the results of using oils daily.

My friend, Sandy said years ago when she first smelled a few of the emotional oils, she did not like them. When her son passed away, I sent her the emotional oils. She said she couldn't get enough of the *Renewing Blend* and *Comforting Blend* blends as well as the *Let It Go* blend listed on page 251.

I feel the essential oils you need at the time are the ones your body says, "*Yes*! Give me some of that."

WHAT are ESSENTIAL OILS?

Essential oils are compounds extracted from plants. The oils capture the plant's scent and flavor, or "essence." Unique aromatic compounds give each essential oil its characteristic essence. Essential oils are obtained through distillation (via steam and/or water) or mechanical methods, such as cold pressing. Essential oils have been used for a very long time, for thousands of years, for medicine.

3 COOL THINGS about ESSENTIAL OILS

The first cool thing about pure essential oils is they're 100% natural and safe. There's nothing added to the oil or taken away from the oil. They're just simply pure oil extracted from the plants with no side effects and no addictions.

They are safe for babies, children, adults, and the elderly. My Nana, who is 103, loves them. Essential oils are extracts from plants and those plants have amazing health benefits.

A pure oil is about fifty to seventy times more powerful than herbs. One drop of pure *Peppermint* essential oil is equivalent to drinking twenty-eight cups of peppermint tea.

So, they're really potent.

What I love about pure essential oils is the CPTG standard. As previously stated, it stands for Certified Pure Tested Grade, and it means the oils are completely pure and potent. Pure means there are no foreign contaminants or fillers. Potent means that each plant was grown in a part of the world where that plant grows best, resulting in the absolute best chemistry for that plant. When you have the ideal natural chemistry, the essential oil extracted does exactly what we want it to do for our health.

For example, my friend deals with headaches. After trying a few drops of peppermint—less than twenty-five cents—on her neck and rubbing into her temples, the headache diminishes and she feels such relief. She also found the headaches weren't happening as much. It's way faster and more effective than her daily *acetaminophen* tablet... and with no side effects.

So, that's the first cool thing about essential oils, they are 100% natural and safe.

Number 2 - They are More Effective than Many Modern Approaches to Health Problems

Let's say first, your body is made up of cells, and we know that cells have oily-cell membranes. The cell membrane protects the cell, it keeps all the good elements in, and all the bad ones out. Now, bacteria and viruses are harmful to our cells. Bacteria usually form on the outside of the cell and viruses duplicate the DNA on the inside of the cell.

All you have to remember is bacteria on the outside, viruses on the inside.

Let's say you went to the doctor with a bacterial infection. What would he recommend for you? (Give you an antibiotic.) And after taking the antibiotic for seven to ten days in most cases, it would probably clear up the infection—but the 'cure' often comes with wreaking havoc on your gut, hormones, and immune system.

Now if you had a virus like the cold or flu, what would he say? (Go home, drink a lot of water, rest and let it run its course.) The reason why is because most of the modern recommendations are water-based synthetic agents—and frequently come with side-effects and addictions. Water and oil don't mix, so if the recommendation from your doctor is water-based, it will have a really hard time penetrating through that oily-cell membrane and stopping the duplication of a virus.

Essential oils are different because they are oil-based, which means they can permeate your cell membranes. They can work on a cellular level without side effects or addictions. They can combat bacteria on the outside of the cell and prevent the duplication of viruses on the inside. That's why they are often more effective than the modern approach to health problems. So Cool, right?

I dealt with constant illnesses—colds and flus every month. My mom alerted me to how often I was down sick with something. After I started to use a blend of *Clove, Cinnamon, Rosemary, Wild Orange*, and *Eucalyptus* oils on a regular basis, I did not have that crazy monthly illness. I felt my immune system boosted and able to handle even seasonal stuff. It was game changing for my body and my life.

Number 3 – Cheaper than Traditional Medical Care

The third cool thing about essential oils is, they are cheaper than traditional medical care.

If your doctor gave you a prescription for an antibiotic, how much would it cost for the prescription?

Even if you don't pay for prescriptions, you still may need to transport to the doctor or take time off work. Let's not even talk about the germ-infested doctor's office and the time you sit waiting to be seen, driving to and from...and so much more of the inconvenience of going to the doctor.

When someone in my family has an ear infection, we rub two drops of *Lavender* and two drops of *Melaleuca* around their ear and put them to bed. Twelve hours later the ear infection is cleared up. It costs us about fifteen cents for that one drop of essential oil. Now whether it costs you $15.00 to $50.00 for the prescription, or whether it costs nothing because maybe you live in a country with free medical care or your insurance rocks, essential oils are still less expensive than the fuel in the car you pay to go to the doctor.

That's not including the half day of work you probably had to take off for this urgent care episode. We also haven't taken into account the fact antibiotics harm your gut, and you might have to buy extra probiotics for two weeks to fix the damage—which is even more money.

Whatever it is, we save hundreds of dollars a year in medical costs because of essential oils. You cannot afford *not* to use natural solutions—*That* is why essential oils are cheaper than traditional medical care.

Lavender essential oil is *Aaaamazing*! It truly is game changing for all. One day my cute nephew was having a two-year-old tantrum moment. His mom took a drop of *Lavender* essential oil, rubbed it in her hands right above his head as he was kicking and screaming on the floor. In a few seconds, his body stopped and he quietly laid there. Then his cute little voice said, "Not da oils."

It was the best moment ever to see how quick even the scent could have such an impact even in that moment.

3 Ways to use Pure Essential Oils

The three ways I use essential oils every day are,

1) Aromatically—take a drop in your hand, rub your hands together and cup your hands under your nose. Make a scent tent. Breathe in three seconds, hold three seconds, exhale three seconds. Got a diffuser? Put some oils in your water diffuser to make a whole room happy and light.

2) Topically—a drop on your wrist and bottom of the feet and you can trust that within a minute the oils will be in your blood stream with positive results.

3) Internally—I love a drop of *Lime* essential oil in my water, or a drop of *Protective Blend* in my orange juice. I also love cooking with the oils. They bring the flavor of my foods to life—aromatherapy for the tongue. Yum!

ESSENTIAL OILS and BRAIN STUDIES

There are so many studies on essential oils and ailments. You can go to *pubmed.gov* to check out all the essential oils studies.

One of my all-time favorite oils is *Frankincense*... it is the baby Jesus oil so it must be a powerful one, right? I love *Frankincense*.

I put a drop of *Frankincense* with a drop of *Wild Orange* in my palm—inhale it—breathe it in... and then take that palm and go from my chin to my heart back up to my chin and feel a shift.

When I started to do this for the first time since my baby died, I felt like I had finally come back to myself...as weird as that sounds, I finally found *me* back in me again.

Those two pure essential oils together actually connect the brain to heart, which feels like an important thing to have connected. I know they were disconnected after my baby died.

The brain trying to analyze it—figure it all out and the heart broken—totally disconnected. The two oils together connected what had been disconnected, to bring one heart to one mind together. PRICELESS.

What can Essential Oils be used for?

Essential oils can be used in so many ways, including natural cleaning. I have many pure essential oil recipes to kick out all those nasty toxic chemical cleaners. I also add pure essential oils to my cooking recipes—a few drops. But I especially love using these pure oils for physical and emotional wellness.

A Look at the Emotional Center of the Brain

One of my favorite ways is using them to support my emotions. A few drops of pure essential oils and I am in a different mindset with positive emotions.

Because of the unique, direct relationship between emotions and olfaction within the brain, essential oils can help "unlock" stored memories and emotions. When you breathe in an essential oil, molecules enter the limbic system and elicit an emotional response releasing from the amygdala.

The limbic system, often referred to as the emotional brain, resides within the cerebrum. This portion of the brain handles emotional response, hormone function, behavior, motivation, long-term memory, and sense of smell. Several other specialized areas reside within the limbic system, including:

- Hippocampus—responsible for forming short-and long-term memories.

- Amygdala—perceives emotions such as anger, fear, and sadness; plays a role in controlling aggression; helps store memories of events and emotions; also plays a role in sexual activity and libido.
- Hypothalamus—controls reproduction, sleep patterns, and body homeostasis.
- Thalamus—relays sensory information to the cerebral cortex.

In addition to being closely tied to the sense of smell, you can see why our emotions can affect so many other things in our lives. The portion of your brain that governs emotions also plays a part in memory, sexual desire, reproduction, sleep, and overall homeostasis.

So How can we Change Our Emotions with Essential Oils?

Remember in Chapter 14 when we talked about Karol Kuhn Truman's book, *Feelings Buried Alive Never Die*?

Remember in Karol's book, it lists the physical ailments and the emotions associated with those physical ailments? It said for *Anxiety* the emotions are: "Feels unable to 'call the shots' in life, Feels boxed in, Feels helpless to affect a change."

Does that not sound like the emotions of losing a baby?

Especially for a control freak, like me. Not a lot of physicians will talk about the emotional aspect of grief that affects us physically. None of mine did.

We are needing to release emotional, to release the physical—which is how that *Grounding Blend* oil affected my anxiety and released it from the body emotionally as well as physically. It was a power play on using the essential oils and releasing from the body. This is how these pure Essential oils work in the systems of the body—powerfully being able to release Emotionally as well as Physically.

Here is where you can purchase Feelings Buried Alive Never Die

A study conducted by the medical universities of Berlin in Germany, and Vienna in Austria in June 1994 confirmed that certain sesquiterpenes can cross the blood-brain barrier.

The blood-brain barrier is a membrane that prevents certain damaging substances like medicine from reaching the brain tissues and cerebrospinal fluid. The barrier can be described as a filter through which only tiny molecules can pass.

Sesquiterpenes, commonly found in essential oils such as *Frankincense*, *Vetiver*, and *Sandalwood*, are known to have the ability to cross this barrier. This molecule allows them to directly interact with brain cells, unlike most pharmaceutical drugs. This is the power of essential oils on your brain and the emotions we carry with our past traumas.

As stated, the brain is a such an interesting and intricate organ, but scientific research has shown emotions actually originate in the limbic system. This system is mainly in charge of processing and formatting memory, smell and, of course, emotions. A gland called the amygdala which plays the primary role in the processing of mind, emotions, decision making, and fight-or-flight response is also located in this system.

A really amazing discovery happened in 1989, by neuroscientist Dr. Joseph LeDoux from New York Medical University, the amygdala is essential for acquisition and storage of memory and expression of fear responses. Therefore, the amygdala is also responsible for storing the emotional trauma.

Remember me finding my baby dead a crib and the emotional impact that must have had on my amygdala? The research found the only way to stimulate this gland—this emotional storing gland, is through the sense of smell—fragrances.

Aroma plays a huge roll in triggering a limbic system response and clearing out that amygdala. So fricken cool, right?

Read more on this amazing research.

This sounds to me like a *huge* breakthrough to treat emotional trauma from our fears, anxieties, and heck of bad experiences we've dealt with or are dealing with in life.

So basically, because of the unique direct relationship between emotions and the olfactory system within the brain, essential oils can help "unlock" stored memories and emotions. When you breathe in an essential oil, molecules enter the limbic system and elicit an emotional response.

An aversion to a particular oil may indicate something more than just personal preference. It could actually be stirring an unpleasant emotional response. Conversely, oils that bring about positive emotions are likely favored. This is because the aromas, the essential oils, will actually affect your emotions. In a positive way, I hope.

Another fascinating scientific study...

OILS to SUPPORT the EMOTIONS

You may be asking, "Where do we begin with what I am dealing with?" I am glad you asked.

There are so many pure essential oils that can help with emotions and whatever you are dealing with. A few examples for now:

- Do you want to feel calm, less agitated, comforted? Try *Lavender, Calmer, Calming Blend, Roman Chamomile, Sandalwood* or *Steadying Blend*.
- Want to let go of anger, upset and feel joyful? Try *Restful Blend, Invigorating Blend, Uplifting Blend, Springtime Blend, Lemon, Cardamom, Geranium, Siberian Fir* or *Melissa*.
- Feeling unstable, insecure, misunderstood? Grab some *Grounding Blend, Clary Calm, Cedarwood, Calming Blend, Black Spruce, Bergamot, Cassia* or *Pink Pepper*.
- Feeling emptiness, grief or loss of will to live? Please use *Vetiver, Respiratory Blend, Comforting Blend, Rose, Hopeful Blend, Melissa* or *Frankincense*.
- Blaming? *Renewing Blend* or my *Let it Go* blend right below this.

My favorites to support my emotions are *Frankincense, Grounding Blend, Invigorating Blend* and *Restful Blend*—game changers for me.

One of my favorite *emotions* books you can buy to use as you figure out what you're feeling and how to assist in shifting those emotions to feel better, to feel alive, and to feel supported/uplifted can be found here:

AromaTools Emotions book

Oils for sleeping can be different for you than what I use to sleep. My body loves *Frankincense* and *Restful Blend* in the diffuser and a few drops over my forehead to shut the mental brain chatter down. I sleep sound.

After my little sister died, my mom was not sleeping. Her doctor put her on a hard sleeping pill. She was on that sleeping pill for years and became fully reliant on it. When I was introduced to essential oils and I found that they worked amazing for me to sleep, I took them to my mom to try. I let her go through them and see what her body loved.

She picked *Lavender*—pure and yummy *Lavender*. A few drops on her pillow, a few drops on her forehead and a few drops in her diffuser and she sleeps all night long. That simple for her.

Sleeping, I would suggest to try *Lavender* or *Restful Blend* or *Roman Chamomile* with *Frankincense* first…but *Calming Blend, Respiratory Blend* and *Marjoram* might work for you.

Supporting your immune system with *pure* Essential oils is also possible. I love *Protective Blend, Oregano, Lemon, Tea Tree, Rosemary, Clove, Cinnamon, Frankincense, Arborvitae* or *Melissa*.

I also love to apply an oil with my spine treatment when I am feeling immune compromised. I start with a few drops of each oil with a one at a time down my spine and bottom of my feet:

Frankincense, a carrier oil (coconut or olive oil) *Tea Tree, Oregano, Protective Blend, Lemon,* and top it with *Peppermint* or *Eucalyptus.*

The essential oil how-to book I love and recommend.

I love combining essential oils and creating blends that support me in whatever I am going through. I have created some blends for you. You just need oil-roller bottles to use the blends.

All Emotional Oils Blend:

10 drops *Renewing Blend*

10 drops *Comforting Blend*

10 drops *Reassuring Blend*

10 drops *Uplifting Blend*

10 drops *Inspiring Blend*

10 drops *Encouraging Blend*

Add to a 10 ml roller bottle and top with *Fractionated Coconut Oil*

We have an amazing emotional release blend that I absolutely love to use to let things go.

It was created by my brother, Tom who was working a booth. A service member who had served four tours, came in asking about PTSD and what oils he could use. My brother gave him a few samples.

When that young man had an attack, he had a thought to grab all the oils and throw them on his body. He said it shut down his PTSD episode.

Upon hearing the soldier's testimony, this beautiful blend was created and has been used for so many people dealing with PTSD, anxiety, emotional outbursts, and so much more.

We call it the *Let It Go* blend. You can say this affirmation as you are applying it: "I find it beneficial for my own good to let go of the things that do not serve me, simply for the reason they are heavy and I am not the one who needs to carry them anymore. I give them to source of all light and love."

Let It Go Blend:

20 drops *Frankincense*—The oil of truth and light.

10 drops *Invigorating Blend*—The oil of childlike, motivated, creativity.

10 drops *Siberian Fir*—The oil of honest perspective, optimistic, wisdom.

One of my favorite blends to assist me to thrive in my life is called the *Thriver* blend. I use this affirmation as I am applying the blend on: "I am strong. I am powerful. I am creative. I am connected. I am healed. I am better than okay. I am a thriver. Everything always works out for me and my highest good."

Thriver blend:

5 drops *Bergamot*— The oil of self-acceptance and love, confident and good enough.

3 drops *Frankincense*—The oil of truth and light, felt loved and connected with the source of all things.

1 drop *Melissa*—The oil of lightened, energized, spiritual connection.

2 drops *Lime*—The oil of zest and love for a courageous life.

2 drops *Ylang Ylang*—The oil of inner child, playful, healing, joyful.

3 drops *Wild Orange*—The oil of abundance and goodness.

1 drops *Siberian Fir*—The oil of honest perspective, optimistic wisdom.

1 drop *Patchouli*—The oil of balanced, confident, physical expression.

1 drop *Arborvitae*—The oil of Divine, peaceful, grounded, trusted grace.

3 drops *Cypress*—The oil of motion and flow, trusting, flexible and adaptable.

2 drops *Spearmint*—The oil of confident, clarity, courageous communication.

The next blend was created for times in my life when I knew I needed to *Rise up* when I was going for something bigger in my life. I love this blend for daily rising up and stepping into my thriving life, like writing this book. As I am applying this yummy blend I say, "I am ready to rise up and shine as I step into my powerful and divinely guided life today. I accept all blessings, opportunities, wealth, goodness, love, prosperity and light into my life."

Rise Up Blend:

3 drops *Lime*—The oil of zest & love for a courageous life.

3 drops *Roman Chamomile*—The oil of guided peaceful, spiritual purpose.

4 drops *Bergamot*—The oil of self-acceptance and love, confident and good enough.

1 drop *Fennel*—The oil of responsibility in tuning into inner self and inner soul wisdom.

1 drop *Ylang Ylang*—The oil of inner child, playful, healing, joyful.

2 drops *Sandalwood*—The oil of sacred, spiritual devotion and clarity, connected to higher being.

3 drops *Doulgas Fir*—The oil of generational healing, wisdom and learning from past.

1 drop *Arborvitae*—The oil of Divine, peaceful, grounded, trusted grace.

3 drops *Litsea*—The oil of inspired, intuitive, trust of inner self, manifesting all possibilities.

3 drops *Wild Orange*—The oil of abundance and goodness.

1 drop *Cassia*—The oil of self courageous and authentic assurance.

Many times in the midst of our grief and even in life, we feel disconnected from humanity. This blend helps me feel connected. I use the affirmation, "I am connected as one with all of humanity and this earths. It feels good to be connected, seen and heard.

<u>CONNECTED BLEND:</u>

2 drops *Basil*—The oil of renewal, regenerated and strengthened.

3 drops *Bergamot*—The oil of self acceptance and love, confident and good enough.

2 drops *Cedarwood*—The oil of community, emotionally connected and supported.

1 drop *Ginger*—The oil of being capable, empowered and committed.

> 2 drops *Kumquat*—The oil of authentic, aligned, sincere presence.
>
> 1 drop *Litsea*—The oil of inspired, intuitive, trust of inner self, manifesting all possibilities.
>
> 1 drop *Marjoram*—The oil of open connection, softhearted and trusting.
>
> 1 drop *Melissa*—The oil of lightened, energized, spiritual connection.
>
> 1 drop *Roman Chamomile*—The oil of guided peaceful, spiritual purpose.
>
> 3 drops *Tangerine*—The oil of gladness, spontaneous, joyful creativity.
>
> 3 drops *Red Mandarin*—The oil of childlike, innocent, positive perspective.

A few months ago, I was in Canada teaching essential oils classes when a darling girl shared a lot of *hard stuff* going in her life.

She shared how she was feeling used and abused by people in her life and how low she felt.

I could see her self-esteem was so off. She was being really hard on herself.

So we sat down and created her a blend of oils...and I played her the song from *The Greatest Showman*, *This Is Me*.

THIS IS ME BLEND:

> 4 drops *Frankincense*—The oil of truth and light felt loved and connected with the source of all things.
>
> 6 drops *Bergamot*—The oil of self-acceptance and love.
>
> 3 drops *Renewing Blend*—Forgiving all and letting go.

- 2 drops *Clove*—The oil of healthy boundaries.
- 2 drops *Lime*—The oil of zest and love for a courageous life.
- 3 drops *Green Mandarin*—The oil of pure potential.
- 4 drops *Grapefruit*—The oil of honoring and loving the body.
- 1-2 drops *Peppermint*—The oil of a buoyant and resilient heart.

That song needs to be blasted and sung loudly, too.

Journaling Thoughts

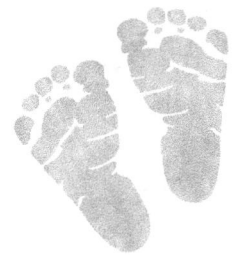

* 26 *

MEDITATING into YOUR GREATNESS

"Meditation is a process of lightening up, of trusting the basic goodness of what we have and who we are, and of realizing that any wisdom that exists, exists in what we already have. We can lead our life so as to become more awake to who we are and what we're doing rather than trying to improve or change or get rid of who we are or what we're doing. The key is to wake up, to become more alert, more inquisitive and curious about ourselves." ~ Pema Chodron

MEDITATION DOES NOT COME EASY for me. My mind goes a gazillion miles-a-minute and shutting it down is not easy at all. Quite A few years ago, my husband, Dirk and I took a trip to Chicago to hang out with Dr Joe Dispenza for a week. Meditation was the only item on our schedule with him that whole week. I did not think I'd be able to do it, to shut down, turn off my phone, and meditate for days into a whole week. Yet I did it.

What I love about Dr Joe is that his meditations are guided—he speaks the whole time, not ever leaving me in my head to run crazy. I love meditating with him. You can google/YouTube him to listen to his profound knowledge and the science of meditating.

He said, "You created the problems in your body with your thoughts, so you can heal them with your thoughts."

I so believe in the power of meditation.

I have created some healing mediations for you to try when you're ready. Deep breathing—or Breath-work—is a form of finding healing and acceptance in your body.

It helps by bringing you into the moment and finding peace.

Thich Nhat Hahn said, "Feelings come and go like clouds in a windy sky, yet conscious breathing is my anchor."

Breathing can be your anchor, too, if you allow it to be. I love playing some Yanni or Enya as I meditate with these. It might take some time to get use to them, but they are powerful for stepping into your new life with your angel and into your new way of being.

My Meditation Gifts for you

Through the years I have done a few mediations that make such a difference for me. I always ground myself in my source and let God's golden light fill me up as I finish the meditation. I hope these work for you. You can record them with your voice with music playing in the voice recorder on your phone so you can have them anytime and anywhere.

Happy meditating.

BEING ONE WITH YOUR ANGEL MEDITATION

Remember the story I shared with you about me realizing that I had my baby chained to me and how I cut my ties, broke the unhealthy chains with my baby to let her go and let her do her mission?

I had to create a positive and healthy connection with her. I wanted a *powerful* connection with her.

I want you to have a loving connection with your angel, too. That is what this meditation is for.

Ready...

I want you to sit comfortably, taking three large deep breaths. First deep breath I want you to breathe in heavenly golden light and exhale negative thoughts or emotions. Next breath, breathe in Celestial light and love, breathe out negative and any darkness in your body. Third breath, breathe in God's eternal and unconditional love and breathe out anything that does not serve a higher connection to God and Angels. Your Angels.

Relax and allow yourself to feel pure light in you. All of you is filled with pure light filling you up. There are no holes in your body. You are allowing pure light to fill up your body. You are filled up with Golden sunshine light.

Breathe...

Now picture a beautiful, large empty meadow. Growing in this meadow are thousands of beautiful wild flowers with grass covering everywhere. It is bright and airy. It's heavenly. It's a great place to stay for a while.

As you stand there, you see your beautiful angel, your Angelic being you want this one connection with. They are standing right in front of you. You see them as the perfect, healthy age heaven allows us to be. Or, however you want to remember them with

God's perfect touch all over them. They are whole, complete, and perfect. No flaws.

Do you see them? Standing in front of you in their perfect, heavenly form?

What does he/she look like? They are beautiful. Pure light. See him/her? Look upon them, Hold their beauty in your eyes.

Now I want you to imagine a beautiful cord of light. Imagine that cord being touched by the hand of God, so it lights up beautifully. Place that cord into your heart and watch that heavenly rope magically go into the heart of your angel. It immediately connects you two as it flows from you into them and brightens up.

You now have this beautiful connection to your angel. That connection is always there and you can call upon them at any time as per this connected lighted gift.

You have a guardian angel. An enabling power available to be there for you for healing, for hope, for direction, for guidance and for further light knowledge.

Breathe all this in, deeply. See this visual of the meadow, your angel, and the lighted cord every day as you heal in the pain and grief of your loss still.

You may step into this daily as you ask for the grace, comfort, and guidance of your angel with this giving connection. Take this visual with you as you come back to your life. Open to receiving light and love in your life.

Take a deep breath and open your eyes.

Back pack dump Meditation

Sit comfortably, taking deep breaths, relaxing and allowing yourself to feel light in you.

I want you to sit comfortably, taking three deep breaths. First deep breath, I want you to breathe in peace and joy. Exhale fear and sadness. Next breath, breathe in hope and love, breathe out anger and negativity. Third breath, breathe in God's eternal and unconditional love and breathe out, letting go of fear, upset and hurt.

Now, I want you to imagine you're standing at the top of a large mountain you just hiked up. You made it to the top of Angel's Landing. It's so raw, real and so beautiful. You made it and you are standing at the top of this mountain looking out at the view, wondering how you made it and why your backpack was so heavy. Why does it feel like you're carrying so much in this backpack? You open it up and see tons of rock—big boulders that you carried up the trail with you.

How did you make it up there with this heavy pack? You can't even believe. You are ultra-strong carrying all of this stuff up.

As you pick up a boulder you notice it's labeled, "I'm not..." What? What does that boulder say? What is it that you have been saying about yourself for a very long time? I'm not pretty enough, smart enough? You have been saying, "I'm not good enough" ...or what, for a long time.

I want you to see the writing on this boulder, words you said about yourself, starting from the time you were young. See the *not* truth on that rock.

Now take that boulder and throw it over the cliff. See it crash into another rock and explode apart. It no longer is a part of you. It's no longer allowed to be carried around with you or in your backpack. You dumped it.

Now take another boulder or rock out and see what is written on it.

"I don't belong, I'm not loved, I'm a bad girl, I don't fit in, I can't do it, I am not liked, I don't have friends, I am not supported, I am all alone."

What do the boulders in your backpack say? Take each one out, see the print on them, one at time. Then throw them over the cliff, one at a time, and watch them crash and break into pieces.

Empty your backpack, dumping each rock off the cliff and seeing that negative thought around your life, the death, and loss and watch those thoughts explode and break up. They don't serve you. Let them go.

As you look out from the top of the beautiful Angel's Landing view, see yourself take in the energy of the amazing view. I want you to stand with your arms wide open like you're about to fly.

As you stand there, call on your angels to show up for you. See your sweet angels surround you, bringing you messages of light and love.

They are saying, "You made it. You got this. You are strong. You are inspiring. You are courageous and full of life. You are a gift to others. You have so much to give and share. You are my hero. I love you. You are light and love."

What are they saying to you right now? What would your angels say to you? What do you need to hear from them?

They are whispering to you. Listen, open up and hear them. Stand with arms open and let the words penetrate into your heart and into your head.

You are on Angel's Landing and they are there telling you what you need to know. Take it in. Let it live in you. Let your heart be open to the messages you are being given. They are for you, and you can use them to make it through. You *do* have this. You *are* strong. You are amazing. You are inspiring. The world needs you. You are whole, complete, and perfect exactly as you.

Even with this experience and that experience, they need you to share and step into this world with your light and your strength.

Ahhhh. Breathe in the air up there. Fill your lungs with it and see yourself fill up with the breath of the angels and their sweet messages. Listen to the messages of the angels. What are they telling you? Remember the sweet messages so you can write them down. They have so much to tell you and so much they want you to know. They have been waiting to whisper to you. Listen up. Breathe it up. Take a deep breath.

Open your eyes and go write the messages spoken to you by the angels and God...

River Meditation

Allow yourself to relax and sit comfortably, taking three deep breaths, inhaling love, exhaling hate. Breathing in goodness, exhaling negative. Breathe in light, exhale dark. Breathe...

I want you to imagine you're sitting next to a beautiful large flowing river. It's so gorgeous there. There are trees all around with flowers. The large serene river flows by you and into a brilliant light tunnel.

As you are sitting next to this river, you see stuff in your head that's not serving you, "I'm not or wasn't enough, I don't belong, I am to blame for this loss, or I did this and caused that" or "I should have been there, done something, said something" or whatever it is.

See this negativity running through your head.

I want you to gather it up, one thought at a time and dump it into the river, let it flow out and away. Then grab another negative thought from your head and dump it into the river and see it flow away. Go for another negative thought in your heart. Anything you are telling yourself that is not light or truth, let that flow out and away into the river. See it flow down. It's no longer in you. Grab another negative thought from your stomach and toss it into the river and see it flow away.

Anymore left? Grab the anger from your liver—it's dark and gloomy. Toss it into the river. See it float away. Gather up all of the negative thoughts in all parts of your body and dump them into the river, letting them flow out and down.

I want you to see a beautiful light tunnel at the end of the river. The whole river is lit up by a powerful energy source. You see someone standing at the bend of the river in light. It is Jesus Christ. He is the source of all light. His amazing light is recycling all the negative energy and all the garbage of thoughts and emotions being dumped into the river. He is turning them into beautiful waves that lighten up, coming back and flowing up to you.

This creates phenomenal energy for the river and is flowing right back around to you.

Now dip your feet into the river and see yourself filling up the void of space the negative thoughts had taken, with good thoughts. See these beautiful thoughts from Christ flow into you, "I am light. I am love. I am hope. I am healing. I am whole, complete and perfect exactly as I am. I am open and loving. I am acceptance. I am truth. I am service. I am one with all. I am loved, I am open to all good."

Fill your mind with the good of the river that flows into you. Filling your mind with the thoughts of the good, the hope and the peaceful ones that flow back to you. You fill your mind with light and truth. You fill your heart with peace and love. You fill your stomach with positivity and generosity. You fill your liver with acceptance and unconditional love.

You see the Light of Christ flow in you and you are whole. You are filled with His light, His love, His healing, His peace,

His Spirit. You breathe it in deeply and you feel whole and fed. Breathe it in.

Open your eyes.

The river is always available for you to sit by anytime you need to dump anything negative and find truth and light. Come back often and find light from the river.

Golden Light Meditation

Sit in a comfortable place in a comfortable position with your feet flat on the ground. Take three deep breaths in and blow them out.

I want you to imagine you can see into heaven, seeing your Heavenly Father standing there with His brilliant light energy and it's so perfect.

This beautiful golden light is pure and flows from Him. I want you to see a lit-up column of light. You see a beautiful hole open up, and a beautiful golden light coming down from above.

The golden light comes down from heaven and right into the top of your head and down your body. It is a healing energy, a soothing energy, an energy ready to flow through you and heal you.

It flows into you. As it flows into you, you see it go to areas of great pain that you have—your heart, for one. The golden beautiful energy fills your heart with healing light straight from God above. You see your heart fill up with the golden, beautiful light.

It fills your heart completely whole and filled. You feel your heart light up.

Then, the energy moves to other places in your body where you feel pain, heartache, and any hurt. The golden light goes into those places and fills up with golden healing light energy. The golden lights fills up your whole body and it feels so good.

You can see it come up and fill into your toes and feet, up your legs, into your core—your stomach, filling up into your chest and your heart, running into your arms and hands, filling up into your neck and up your head and flowing back up to heaven, until your whole body is filled with beautiful golden celestial light, amazing God healing energy. It fills your whole being, and you feel it heal you.

The light creates peace, love, hope and golden beautiful light in you. It fills your whole being and it feels so yummy. It feels so good.

You are filled with golden light straight from Heaven, straight from God above and it is filling you up, creating a wholeness in you. It fills the voids. It fills the loneliness. It fills the heartache. It fills the grief. It fills the loss of your loved one(s). You are filled with golden beautiful light and it heals you. Filling up your whole soul. You are given this light because you are light. You are loved from this light. You feel the light in you. It's a protective light. It does not allow anything in that does not serve you.

The light protects your precious energy, your open and loving heart, your special soul, and keeps you filled up with golden light, love, and hope.

Stepping into your future is a big deal after big loss. This light assists you in stepping into your future and feel assisted in doing so. You are filled with healing light and you have access to it anytime you want. You can also use the light as a simple light barrier to keep people away who maybe don't serve you at this time or those who don't honor your healing journey.

You are filled with light for you highest good. The light is never ending. It comes from God and it is endless as it flows into you as you wish. It is a gift of healing light and it is yours as often and as much as you would like. Step into it. Honor the light and hold on to the light throughout your moments of the day. You are the golden light. You are one with the golden light. It loves being in you and filling you.

Take a deep breath. Fill up your body with light and air. Breathe it out.

Open your eyes...

The more regularly and the more deeply you meditate, the sooner you will consistently come from a center of love, peace and light, healing your whole being.

As I meditated one day, I saw my Angel with me. I saw her flying with me. It was a beautiful meditation.

This is the song that came into my mind:

Ariann, you are *The Wind Beneath My Wings*.

Forever and ever...

Journaling Thoughts

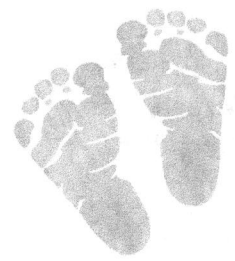

* 27 *

It is Well with My Soul

When peace like a river attendeth my way, when sorrows like sea billows roll. Whatever my lot, Thou hast taught me to say, It is well, it is well with my soul. It is well (it is well). With my soul (with my soul). It is well, it is well with my soul. ~ Horatio Spafford

As I sit and ponder all the experiences the death of my sweet baby, Ariann and my amazing sister, Rebecca have given me, I am in awe. As I look back and finish up this book, I am in awe. My *grief journey* has not been so much different than so many others—others who did it long ago or the same time I did or who are still walking it…or starting it right now.

Facing our grief seems like a frightening journey into a foreign land, a dark and scary trail. We wonder how we can possibly make it and survive it.

I lately have been hearing the term, "the dark night of the soul." We find ourselves in unfamiliar territory and that is super scary. We feel alone whether we have a companion or tribe or not. This will not last.

Within days or maybe months, light will shine around us and we will feel less lost. With the passage of time, maybe months into years, we move back into daylight with dark nights becoming less dark.

There are no timelines for our grief period. Someday *that dark night of the soul* becomes the lesson of your life. We give ourselves permission to live fully, to love fully, and to move on despite the fact our loved one is not physically with us.

The best tribute to our loved one is to *live* again. TO TRULY LIVE. No regrets…

Dr Wayne Dyer says, "Don't die with your music still in you. Don't die with your purpose unfulfilled. Don't die feeling as if your life has been wrong. Don't let that happen to you."

This true story is a powerful way to end this book. This story and song were shared by the Tabernacle Choir in a Christmas performance.

Horatio had an awakening experience to know he was meant to be alive. Anna also heard a voice say to her, "You were spared for a reason, Anna. You have a work to do still."

Perhaps we cannot always say everything is well in all aspects of our lives. There will always be storms to face, and sometimes there will be tragedies. But with faith in a loving God and with trust in His Divine help, we can confidently say, "It is well, it is well with my soul."

I now can sing those words and trust confidently, knowing a loving God has me and it is well with my soul.

The only source of true and solid peace I've found in my life comes from and through the Savior, Jesus Christ. He is the Reason for all seasons. He is the source of true healing. He is the one who bears it all. Through Him, my grief was eased and lightened. Through Him, all grief can be taken. When I finally stepped in to Him, I found the Prince of Peace. I found the Hope of Hopes. I found Ariann, my angel girl.

There is a time to mourn, a time to be silent, and a time for peace and healing. Through Jesus Christ we can heal all that we mourn.

> *Angels, shepherds, and Wise Men sought and found peace from their faith in Jesus Christ. So will you. The Savior's birth is the gift that makes it possible for the Father to give us 'peace in this world, and eternal life in the world to come.'* ~ Henry B Eyring

Ironically, on that Christmas morning, many new stars ago, He was born. I know that because He was born and He loved us enough to die for us and be resurrected to live again, that she lives. My sweet baby lives and because of Him, Rebecca lives. All who have died live. They are alive because of Jesus Christ. I will see Ari again. I will hold her again. I will have all that is promised to me again. Because of Jesus Christ. I know He lived, He loved, He healed, He died, and He lives again.

I don't know all things. I have much to learn and much to grow through. I do know she is with me and she knows so much more than I do. She goes on in my life because Jesus did what He was destined to do in this life. So must I. I have a mission. I have a responsibility to God to do what I said I would do.

I wrote a letter to Ariann the year after she died. In that letter, I told her how much I love her. How honored I was to be her mother, as humbling as that felt. I told her I would see her again, and I would cherish the moments I felt her in my life.

Revelation 21:4 says, "And God shall wipe away all tears from their eyes; and there shall be no more death, neither sorrow, nor crying, neither shall there be any more pain: for the former things are passed away."

I truly look forward to that day. To have no more crying, no sorrow, with fresh eyes to see all. I look back at the heartache, the sorrow, the pain that seemed as it would never end—it has subsided, eased, and I have made it through the roughest part of it, I pray. Yet, to have all of it pass away and hold on to her, is what I hold on to now. I want to hold her again in my arms, to see the beautiful angelic light in her eyes again and to never be apart from her.

A statement by Joseph Smith sits next to a picture of Ariann on my desk: "All your losses will be made up to you in the resurrection, provided you continue faithful. By the vision of the Almighty I have seen it."

What does this mean? All losses will be made up to me. That's a pretty clear and beautiful promise that I have held on to since I can remember.

I love the Nativity scene. I love seeing the many ways Mary, Joseph, Jesus Christ, and those who came are shown and depicted. From the time I came to have a precious Christmas sixteen years ago, where my baby showed back up in a tender moment, I knew the Nativity represented it all for me.

Crazy at it sounds, I came to know that I was also there. I saw that birth and I sang hallelujah as He was born.

I humbly share before you in this beautiful moment my testimony to you.

I absolutely love the Christmas time of year now. I love the gift of the seasons together—the gift of being reminded to be grateful. Gathering with ones we love, with food and fun to the gift of His birth and Christmas, and the Spirit it brings with all its gifts—connecting deeper with others, the music, the decorations, the lights, the trees, the nativities, and All that it is.

Yet, you know I haven't always loved it. On that day thirty-one-plus years ago when our baby girl left and went back to heaven the early hours of Christmas morning—you know I was devastated. Broken. Really pissed off. I blamed a God whom I really didn't know so well, at twenty-one. I was angry at Him for a long, long time.

I spent many years avoiding seasons, especially Christmas and all that it means because of my deep hurt…

I did not know the Power of God and the Gift of the Atonement in my life. Until that one Christmas fourteen years after she had passed away, I had that beautiful, spiritual gift given to me. A few moments of her in the week of that Christmas shifted my whole being around the season.

That one Christmas I truly found her in a moment of *hope* and unconditionally love. What I know is that His birth changed it all for me. For us. He was born in the humblest of all settings, to a virgin mother, with a man who vowed to take care of them on a glorious night, that others actually saw signs and Him at His birth!

As stated in scripture,

> *And behold, he shall be born of Mary, at Jerusalem which is the land of our forefathers, she being a virgin, a precious and chosen vessel, who shall be overshadowed and conceive by the power of the Holy Ghost, and bring forth a son, yea, even the Son of God.*
>
> *And he shall go forth, suffering pains and afflictions and temptations of every kind; and this that the word might be fulfilled which saith he will take upon him the pains and the sicknesses of his people.*
>
> *And he will take upon him death, that he may loose the bands of death which bind his people; and he will*

> *take upon him their infirmities, that his bowels may be filled with mercy, according to the flesh, that he may know according to the flesh how to succor his people according to their infirmities.* (Alma 7:10)

I love this scripture Alma shares with us. Alma knew this truth and so did I—That 'He may *know* according to the flesh *how* to succor His people.'

The Savior's birth, life, Gift of the Atonement, and Resurrection gave Him the power to strengthen us in our trials and even deliver us from them.

In 1838, the Prophet Joseph Smith declared, "The fundamental principles of our religion are the testimony of the Apostles and Prophets, concerning Jesus Christ, that He died, was buried, and rose again the third day, and ascended into Heaven; and all other things which pertain to our religion are only appendages to it."

He lives. He knows me. He felt it all. He bore it *all*. This was the access through which I journeyed to find my own healing, to find acceptance of my *great* loss, to find peace and to find strength to go on. Even in the seasons. Even on Christmas days.

It was through Him, my Savior Jesus Christ that I found her again. That I'll have her again. Be with her again. The best thing to heal my wounded heart, was tapping into the *enabling power* of the Atonement of Jesus Christ. My many *tender mercies*, I believe, came because I finally turned to Him, believed in Him, and sought after Him.

Elder Uchtdorf said,

> *So, when you are encompassed by sorrows and grief, behold the Man. When you feel lost or forgotten, behold the Man.*
>
> *When you are despairing, deserted, doubting, damaged, or defeated, behold the Man.*

He will comfort you. He will heal you and give meaning to your journey. He will pour out His Spirit and fill your heart with exceeding joy. He gives "power to the faint; and to them that have no might he increaseth their strength.

What I did not know at twenty-one when my baby died, was that the gift of that day was really about the power of delivering me from my trials. It was already set in place and ready for me to step into it, no matter what. No matter me.

I did not turn in to it at the time of Ari's death. I turned away. It didn't matter. He still bore it. All of it. He stood ready for me to turn in to Him when I was ready. Yet, He has always turned to me.

The gift of that glorious season comes because He lived, because He died, Atoning for us and because He was resurrected—Creating life for us. Even beyond this life. Truly, there is no other way to heal the wounds of broken relationships or of a fractured society than for each of us to more fully emulate the Prince of Peace.

Isaiah 9:6 says, "For unto us a child is born, unto us a son is given: and the government shall be upon his shoulder: and his name shall be called Wonderful, Counselor, The mighty God, The everlasting Father, The Prince of Peace."

And because he lives, she lives. Because He lives, Rebecca lives. Because He lives, all who have gone from this life live. Because He lives, we all will live, reunited with those we love.

It means I will hold my baby again as a baby. I will see her first steps, watch her walk and run. She will drive a car, play softball, go to a prom, go on a mission. I will see her fall in love and get married. I will see her have children and I will have *lots* of grandbabies. I will watch her grow and flourish in a time of peace and ease. All *will* be made up to me, I KNOW THIS TO BE TRUE. I accept this and look forward to that moment.

I Know that My Redeemer Lives is a powerful song that leaves me in tears every time I sing it, hear it sung, or even read the words. I hear the promises of this song, and I accept them.

My testimony to you is that, "He lives! He knows us. He is there. Our prayers are heard. He answers them. In time, and when we weep, He and the Angels of Heaven weep with us. And He heals all wounds despite us."

May the spirit of this season touch your hearts and may you know, He is not just the Reason for this Season (Christmas), He is the reason for *all* seasons. He is the reason for *all* of life.

Peace be unto you and may you find Peace, a time to mourn and a time to heal…this is my prayer for ya'll…

With love,
Maree

Final Journaling Thoughts

Maree Cottam VanDerzee

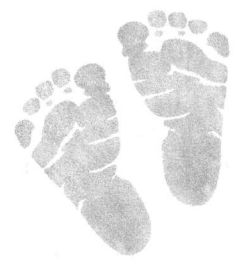 

About the Author

Maree Cottam VanDerzee has a great love for life, now. She is grateful for her experiences and people who've brought her to this point in her life.

She has a tender and beautiful relationship with her Father in Heaven. She knows she is Divinely guided by Him and is so grateful for His all-knowing Hand that leads her.

Maree is a wife to her soul mate, Dirk, for whom she waited a very long time, and he was *so worth* the wait.

She is a mother of three beautiful girls—one of those girls in heaven as her guardian soul angel.

Maree comes from a large family—seven brothers, four sisters, and a gazillion nieces and nephews and greats whom she loves and adores.

Maree loves writing, speaking, and sharing her stories. She is an introvert with a side of extrovert in her that thrives in one-on-ones, smaller events, as well as on stage in large groups speaking her heart.

She loves plants and gardening, passionately sharing about essential oils, and spending time with her family.

And, she loves food!

Maree and her hubby live in Texas. They love to travel in their motor home sharing their passions and empowering others to find freedom in and from themselves.

She believes the soul is great in the site of God and she wants to give everyone that message for themselves.

Connect with Maree:

www.ingramcontent.com/pod-product-compliance
Lightning Source LLC
Chambersburg PA
CBHW050312120526
44592CB00014B/1884